CRIME SCENE

True-Life Forensic Files

D1022487

DISCARDED FROM
GARFIELD COUNTY PUBLIC
LIBRARY SYSTEM

Garfield County Libraries
Parachute Branch Library
244 Grand Valley Way
Parachute, CO 81635
(970) 285-9870 Fax (970) 285-7477
www.garfieldlibraries.org

Copyright © 2008 by Scholastic Inc.

All rights reserved. Published by Scholastic Inc., *Publishers since 1920.*
SCHOLASTIC and associated logos are trademarks and/or registered
trademarks of Scholastic Inc.

No part of this publication may be reproduced, stored in a retrieval system, or
transmitted in any form or by any means, electronic, mechanical, photocopying,
recording, or otherwise, without written permission of the publisher. For information
regarding permission, write to Scholastic Inc., Attention: Permissions Department,
557 Broadway, New York, NY 10012.

The material in this book originally appeared in the following titles in the Scholastic
series **24/7: Science Behind the Scenes/Forensic Files:** *Killer at Large! Criminal
Profilers and the Cases They Solve* and *Killer Wallpaper: True Cases of Deadly
Poisonings.*

Library of Congress Cataloging-in-Publication Data available

ISBN-13: 978-0-545-09231-9
ISBN-10: 0-545-09231-0

10 9 8 7 6 5 4 3 2 1   08 09 10 11 12

Interior design: Red Herring Design/NYC
Additional design: Kay Petronio

Printed in the U.S.A.   23
First printing, September 2008

CRIME SCENE

True-Life Forensic Files

PROFILERS
AND POISON

By D. B. Beres and Anna Prokos

SCHOLASTIC

CONTENTS

FORENSIC 411

Here's the 411 on what criminal profilers really do.

FEDERAL BUREAU OF INVESTIGATION
UNITED STATES DEPARTMENT OF JUSTICE

JANE DOE

SUPERVISORY SPECIAL AGENT

Office of the Director
Federal Bureau of Investigation

These cases are 100% real. Find out how criminal profilers helped solve these mysteries.

17

Case #1:
The Case of the Mad Bomber

A series of bombings terrorizes New York City and baffles the police. Can a criminal profiler help find the bomber?

A serial bomber is nabbed in New York City.

Case #2:
The Case of the Too-Hot Fire

29

Firefighters discover a body inside a burning house, and a profiler takes the case.

Investigators are called after a suspicious fire in Florida.

A computer profiler tracks a hacker in Montreal, Quebec.

37

Case #3:
The Case of the Mysterious Hacker

A university's computer network is under attack. Can a cyber-profiler find the hacker?

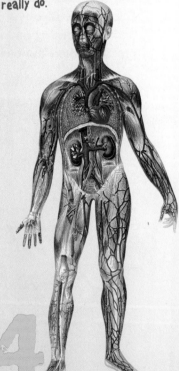

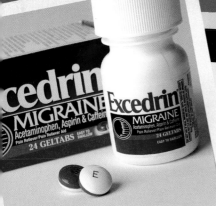

Someone in Washington put poison in this painkiller.

These cases are 100% real. Find out how toxicologists helped solve some poisonous mysteries.

67

Case #4:
The Case of the Deadly Drug

Two people are dead after taking a common pain medicine. Who could have poisoned the pills?

77

Case #5:
The Case of the Poisoned Politician

One night, Viktor Yushchenko is battling for the presidency of Ukraine. The next day, he is fighting for his life.

Was a presidential candidate in Ukraine poisoned?

The emperor may have died from arsenic poisoning.

87

Case #6:
The Case of the Royal Poisoning

French Emperor Napoleon Bonaparte dies after a strange illness. Can a lock of hair solve this historical mystery?

FORENSIC DOWNLOAD

Here's even more amazing stuff about forensic toxicology for you to swallow.

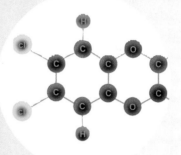

98
FLASHBACK
Key Dates in Forensic Toxicology

100
REAL STUFF
Name Your Poison

104
CAREERS
Help Wanted: Forensic Toxicologist

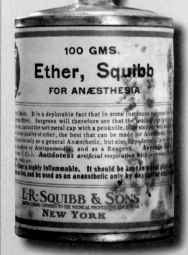

100 GMS.
Ether, Squibb
FOR ANÆSTHESIA

...Oxide. It is a deplorable fact that in some instances our case form Ether. Surgeons will therefore see that the sealing cap is in..., cut out the soft metal cap with a penknife, that stopper we... pure quality of ether, the best that can be made for Anæsthesia... ...not only as a general Anæsthetic, but also hypodermically or... Analeptic or Antispasmodic, and as a Reagent. Average Do... ...(1 Cc.). **Antidotes:** *artificial respiration* with insertion of... ...fresh air.
...Ether is highly inflammable. It should be kept in a cool place... ...the air, and be used as an anaesthetic only by daylight or elsewhere...

E.R. SQUIBB & SONS
MANUFACTURING CHEMISTS TO THE MEDICAL PROFESSION SINCE 1858
NEW YORK

YELLOW PAGES

What happens when a crime is committed and there isn't much evidence? How do police begin to find a suspect?

FORENSIC 411

Anyone could have done it, right? *Wrong.* Criminal profilers can help narrow down the search. Before you get too psyched and jump ahead, read this section.

In this section:

▶ how CRIMINAL PROFILERS really talk;

▶ what kind of PEOPLE they are;

▶ who else is working the CRIME SCENE.

In Your Head

Criminal profilers have their own way of speaking. Find out what their vocabulary means.

suspect
(SUHS-pekt) someone thought to be responsible for a crime

psychology
(sye-KOL-uh-gee) the scientific study of the human mind and human behavior

"This doesn't look like an accident. I'd say we've got ourselves a homicide."

homicide
(HOM-uh-side) a murder

"Profilers aren't magicians. They just know their psychology. They can tell us a lot about our suspect."

"Psycho" has to do with the mind.

"Ology" means "the study of."

criminology
(KRIM-un-OL-uh-gee) the scientific study of crime, criminals, and criminal behavior. An expert in criminology is called a *criminologist*.

"We need an expert in criminology for this case, because the facts don't make sense."

"See if you can get someone in criminal profiling down here to the crime scene."

criminal profiling

(KRIM-uh-nul PRO-file-ing) the use of crime scene evidence and psychology to predict a criminal's personality and habits

"At first glance, this looks like a random crime. But I want to see if there was a motive here."

motive

(MOH-tiv) a reason for doing something

"I want to know what his behavior means."

behavior

(bih-HAYV-yer) the way a person acts or responds to certain conditions. Behavioral sciences are sciences that study the way people behave.

Say What?

Here's some other lingo a profiler might use on the job.

MO

(EM-oh) a term for how a criminal operates. It's short for *modus operandi*. That's Latin for "method of operation."

"The guy has the same **MO** *every time he robs a bank."*

perp

(purp) a person who has committed a crime. It's short for *perpetrator*.

"Don't worry. We're going to catch this **perp** *and put him in jail."*

stats

(stats) official numbers about events that have happened in the past. It's short for *statistics*.

"According to the **stats***, the number of violent crimes has decreased since 1994."*

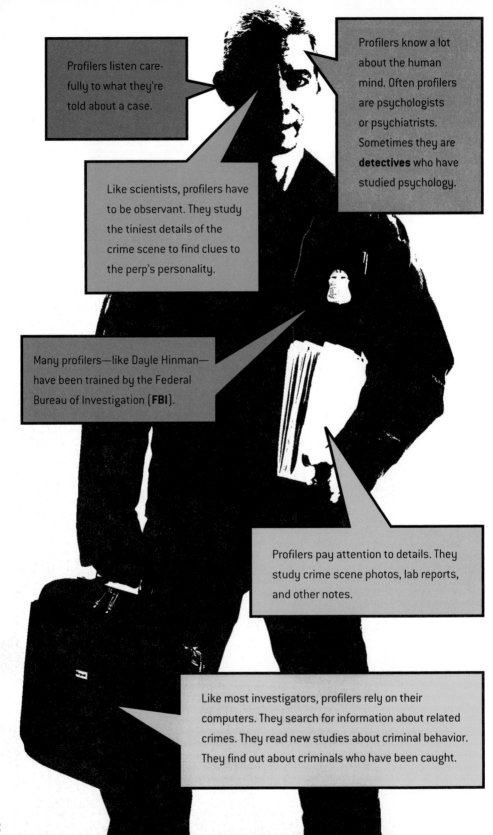

Profilers listen carefully to what they're told about a case.

Profilers know a lot about the human mind. Often profilers are psychologists or psychiatrists. Sometimes they are **detectives** who have studied psychology.

Like scientists, profilers have to be observant. They study the tiniest details of the crime scene to find clues to the perp's personality.

Many profilers—like Dayle Hinman—have been trained by the Federal Bureau of Investigation (**FBI**).

Profilers pay attention to details. They study crime scene photos, lab reports, and other notes.

Like most investigators, profilers rely on their computers. They search for information about related crimes. They read new studies about criminal behavior. They find out about criminals who have been caught.

Profile of a Profiler

What do profilers do, and how do they do it?

Most criminals don't drop **ID** cards at the scene of a crime. Many don't leave fingerprints or **DNA evidence**. But to a good profiler, everything a criminal does is evidence.

Profilers look at the details of a crime. From those details they try to describe the criminal. "Profilers narrow the field of suspects," says Dayle Hinman. She has done profiling work for 26 years.

Are police looking for a man or a woman? Is their suspect angry, or cool and calculating?

Steps to Creating a Profile

▶ Profilers' first step is to gather information. Profilers look at crime scene photos. They study all details of the crime. They get to know the victim.

▶ Next, they look at statistics about solved crimes. They ask what type of person has done this kind of crime in the past. Bombers, for instance, tend to be men. Poisoners tend to be women.

▶ The profiler then pulls the information together to create a profile of the criminal.

What kind of person makes a good profiler? Take a look at the profile on the left.

The Forensic Team

Criminal profilers work as part of a team. Here's a look at some of the experts who help solve crimes.

Forensic DNA Specialists

They collect DNA from traces of body fluids, hair, or skin left at the scene. Then they use this evidence to identify victims and suspects.

Criminal Profilers

They study the details of a crime and create a profile, or description, of the criminal.

DETECTIVES OR AGENTS

They direct the crime investigation. They collect information about the crime, interview witnesses, identify suspects—and arrest them if there's enough evidence!

Trace Evidence Specialists

They collect trace evidence at the scene. That includes fibers, tire tracks, shoe prints, and more. Can this evidence lead them to a criminal?

Medical Examiners

They're medical doctors who investigate suspicious deaths. They try to find out when and how someone died. They often direct other members of the team.

TRUE-LIFE
CASE FILES!

24 hours a day, 7 days a week, 365 days a year, criminal profilers are solving mysteries.

In this section:

▶ how a MAD BOMBER was caught 16 years after he planted his first bomb;

▶ how a PROFILER led police to an arsonist and murderer;

▶ how a profiler discovered A PLOT to steal military secrets over the Internet!

Behind the Scenes

Here's how criminal profilers get the job done. What does it take to solve a crime? Good profilers don't just make guesses. They're like scientists. They follow a step-by-step process.

As you read the case studies, you can follow along with them. Keep an eye out for the icons below. They'll clue you in to each step along the way.

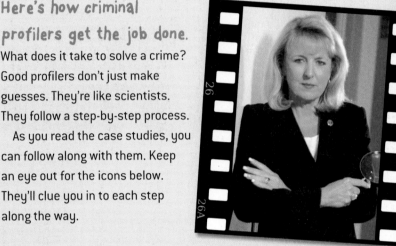

THE QUESTION
At the beginning of each case, the profilers identify **one or two main questions** they need to answer.

THE EVIDENCE
Their next step is to **gather and analyze evidence**. Profilers collect as much information as they can. They study it to figure out what it means.

THE CONCLUSION
Along the way, profilers come up with theories to explain what happened. They test these theories against the evidence. Does the evidence back up the theory? **If so, they've reached a conclusion**.

CRIME SCENE D

The Case of the Mad Bomber

A series of bombings terrorizes New York City and baffles the police. Can a criminal profiler help find the bomber?

New York, New York
December 2, 1956

The Bomber Is Back

A bomb explodes in a New York City theater, and police are stumped.

It was December 2, 1956. There were only three weeks until Christmas. Holiday shoppers bustled along the streets of Brooklyn. Then, at 7:55 P.M., a loud blast shook the ground. Smoke poured out of the Paramount movie theater. A crowd ran out in panic.

The Mad Bomber had struck again!

Everyone in New York knew about the bomber. He'd been planting bombs in the city for 16 years. No one had been killed. But the Paramount bombing injured six people.

Each of the Mad Bomber's **devices** was more powerful than the last. It seemed only a matter of time before someone was killed.

Yet police still had no real clues to the bomber's identity. They knew he had some technical training. His bombs were complex and hard to build. They even

The Paramount movie theater in Brooklyn, New York. This photo was taken in 1956. On December 2, a bomb exploded inside the theater. It had been placed by the Mad Bomber.

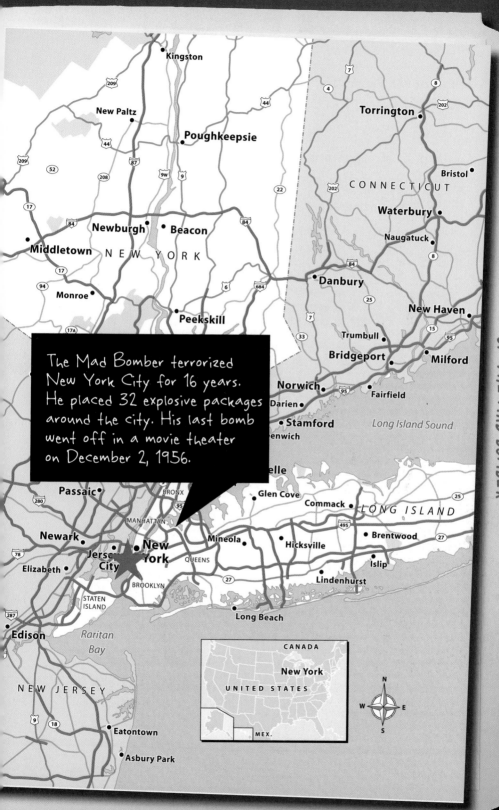

The Mad Bomber terrorized New York City for 16 years. He placed 32 explosive packages around the city. His last bomb went off in a movie theater on December 2, 1956.

had notes from the bomber. Each time he struck, he left a letter written in block letters. He signed each letter, "F.P."

But after 16 years, they had no idea where to look for "F.P." They were desperate. An inspector in the New York City crime lab decided to try something new. He paid a visit to a criminal psychiatrist named Dr. James Brussel.

Psychiatrist or Detective?

Can a psychiatrist look into the mind of the bomber?

In 1956, criminal profilers were almost unheard of. But Dr. James Brussel had studied criminal behavior for years. He had read about the Mad Bomber. Like everyone else in New York City, he had wondered who the person might be. But when the inspector called, Brussel was surprised. He didn't think he could add much to the case.

Still, Brussel agreed to try. The inspector handed over the bomber's case file. Dr. Brussel opened the file and began studying the Mad Bomber.

Dr. Brussel asked himself: How did the bomber behave? And what did that behavior say about the kind of person he is?

Dr. James Brussel was brought in to help solve the Mad Bomber case. He is holding his book *Casebook of a Crime Psychiatrist*. In it, he talks about his role in the case.

CASEBOOK OF A CRIME PSYCHIATRIST

HOW + WHY = WHO

To a profiler, criminals reveal who they are by what they do.

Profilers look at a criminal's behavior in order to get a picture of the person. Here's how it's often done.

1. Staging: What exactly happened at a crime scene? Did the criminal arrange anything deliberately?

2. MO: How does the criminal perform the crimes? What are the patterns to his behavior? Is he calm and careful? Or does he act on impulse?

3. Motive: Why is the criminal committing the crime? Was it revenge? Anger? To make money?

4. Signature Behaviors: What does this criminal do that seems to be particularly important to him?

5. Victimology: If there are victims of the crimes, who are they? Why would the criminal target these particular people?

Sixteen Years of Terror

Dr. Brussel learns the Mad Bomber's history.

The Mad Bomber planted his first bomb on November 16, 1940. He left it on a windowsill at the Consolidated Edison building in New York. Con Edison supplies energy for New York City.

The bomb never exploded. Detectives found a note on the device. It read, "Con Edison crooks, this is for you." Detectives were confused. If the bomb had exploded, the note would have been destroyed. Did the builder purposely make the bomb a dud?

Police found no fingerprints or clues at Con Edison. After a while, no one thought much about it. Then, several months later, the bomber struck again. He left a new device a few blocks from another Con Edison office. This one was wrapped in an old sock. It didn't explode either.

This is a Con Ed plant in the New York area. The Mad Bomber seemed to be angry with this energy company.

The Mad Bomber planted two bombs in Radio City Music Hall. At the time, it was one of the largest indoor theaters in the world. Two people were injured in an explosion there in 1954.

Three months later, the U.S. joined World War II (1939–1945). The bomber sent a letter to the police. The words were cut from newspapers and pasted onto the page. "I will make no more bomb units for the duration of the war," it read. When the war was over, the bombings would start again, he warned. Con Edison must pay for their "**dastardly** deeds."

For the next nine years, no bombs were found. But the bomber kept sending letters. All the notes were signed, "F.P."

On March 29, 1950, an unexploded bomb turned up in New York's Grand Central Terminal. It was similar to the earlier bombs but more powerful and complex.

Another of the bomber's targets was New York's Grand Central Terminal. The bomber placed a total of five bombs in this railroad station.

Then a bomb exploded in a phone booth at the New York Public Library. Another exploded at Grand Central Terminal. Over the next six years, the Mad Bomber planted dozens of bombs. Finally, the Paramount Theater bombing led police to Dr. Brussel.

Creating the Profile

After studying the bomber's crimes, Dr. Brussel created a surprisingly specific profile.

Dr. Brussel carefully studied the evidence in the Mad Bomber's case file. He also used his own knowledge of criminal behavior. Then he developed theories about the evidence.

Theory: The bomber was male.
Evidence: According to statistics, bomb builders are usually male.

Theory: The bomber probably worked at Con Edison in the past.
Evidence: He criticized Con Edison in his angry letters.

Theory: The bomber was paranoid. That's the strong feeling that someone is after you.
Evidence: The bomber believed that Con Edison was out to get him.

Theory: The bomber was about 50 years old.
Brussel's reasoning: Usually, **paranoia** peaks around age 35. The bomber planted his first bomb in 1940. If he were 35 then, he'd be about 50 in 1956.

Theory: The bomber was neat and skilled.
Evidence: He wrote his notes neatly. And the bombs were complex and carefully built.

Theory: The bomber had a high school education but did not go to college.
Evidence: He had probably learned the perfect handwriting in school. But his odd, stuffy language sounded self-taught.

Theory: The bomber was probably from Eastern or Central Europe.
Evidence: Protesters in Eastern and Central Europe have a history of using bombs.

Theory: The bomber lived in Connecticut.
Evidence: Many Eastern and Central Europeans lived in Connecticut. Also, some of the letters had been mailed from a location between Connecticut and New York City.

THE CONCLUSION Dr. Brussel had his profile, and he handed it over to the police. The bomber, he said, was a neat, middle-aged, paranoid Eastern European man from Connecticut.

Brussel went even further. The bomber, he said, would be dressed neatly. "When you catch him, he'll be wearing a double-breasted suit—and it will be buttoned."

Searching for a Madman

Dr. Brussel told the police to release the profile to the media. He wanted the bomber to read about himself in the newspaper. The bomber enjoyed his game with the police. If the profile were wrong, he might brag about it in another letter. Eventually, he could get cocky and make a mistake.

The bomber soon proved Dr. Brussel right. After reading about the profile, he sent more letters to the media. He even called Dr. Brussel, but hung up quickly. In one of his letters, the bomber told about an accident he'd had at work. Detectives knew they were getting close.

Meanwhile, police gave the profile to Con Edison. A clerk searched their files for employees who fit the profile. Eventually, she found a file that looked promising. A man named George Metesky had been injured on the job. When he got sick with tuberculosis, he blamed it on the accident. He filed a claim for disability, asking Con Edison to pay him money. The company refused to pay.

Metesky then wrote angry letters to Con Edison. He mailed them from his home in Waterbury, Connecticut.

In one of the letters, he promised to take revenge for the company's "dastardly deeds."

The clerk handed over the file to her boss. Her boss passed it to the police. They compared the details of the accident with the story the bomber told in his letter. They matched perfectly. Thanks to Dr. Brussel, detectives finally had their man.

EVIDENCE

When investigators searched his garage, they found materials for more bombs.

Left: George Metesky's garage in Waterbury, Connecticut.

Caught!

Police arrest the Mad Bomber. He matches the profile perfectly—right down to the suit.

George Metesky lived in Waterbury with his two sisters. Neighbors described him as polite and neatly dressed.

After his arrest, George Metesky posed for photographers. Underneath his overcoat, his double-breasted suit was neatly buttoned.

But he kept to himself. He went to New York City often. He attended Catholic mass. Beyond that, his neighbors knew little about him.

They were stunned when police came to Metesky's door. He greeted officers in his bathrobe. Right away, he confessed to being the bomber. He said that F.P. stood for "Fair Play."

Police allowed Metesky to change into street clothes. He put on a double-breasted suit—and it was buttoned!

At his trial, a jury found Metesky to be insane. The judge sent him to a mental hospital.

Dr. Brussel became famous. The New York City police often called him for help on important cases. His work helped give profilers a role in police departments around the world. After all, he described the Mad Bomber— right down to the clothes on his back.

In this case, a profiler looked at several crimes to get a profile of the perp. What can a profiler do with only one crime? Find out in the next case.

The Case of the Too-Hot Fire

firefighters
discover a body
inside a burning
house, and a
profiler takes
the case.

TRUE-LIFE CASE #2

Edgewater, Florida
January 23, 1991
9:36 A.M.

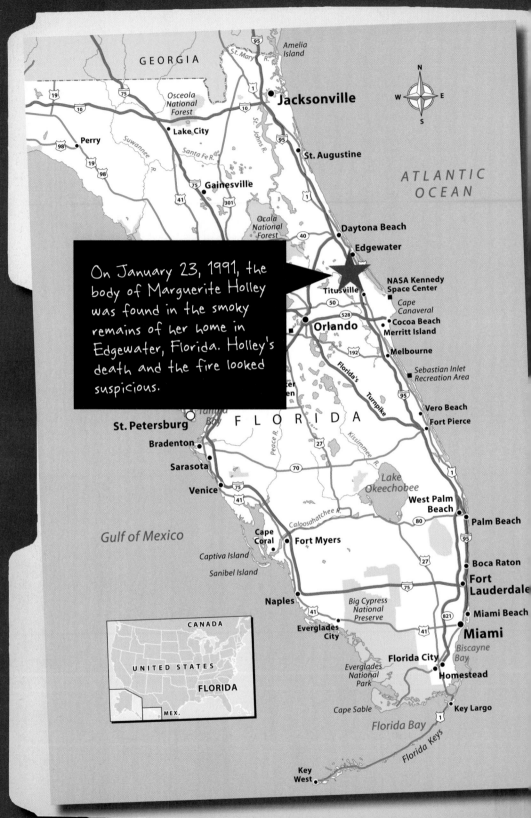

On January 23, 1991, the body of Marguerite Holley was found in the smoky remains of her home in Edgewater, Florida. Holley's death and the fire looked suspicious.

Fire!

A house goes up in flames—with a dead body inside.

At first it looked like a sad accident. Fire broke out in a house in Edgewater, Florida. It happened on the morning of January 23, 1991. Firefighters arrived on the scene and battled the flames. When they got the blaze under control, they entered the house. In the bedroom they found its owner, already dead on the floor.

The body belonged to Marguerite Holley, a grandmother and retired nurse. Next to her was a broken oil lamp. The fire had burned a hole in the floor.

At first glance, it seemed obvious what had happened. The oil lamp fell and set the floor on fire. The fire spread quickly and trapped Holley.

But as police looked around, a different story took shape. Holley's car was missing from the garage. Could it have been stolen? Glass had been broken out of a back-door window. Was that where the thief had entered the house?

An oil lamp like this one was found next to the body of Marguerite Holley. Had it caused the fire in her house?

Then there was the position of Holley's body. She lay flat on her back, arms at her sides. She didn't look like she had been fighting for her life. Finally,

A fireman waits at Marguerite Holley's house for a police detective. The firemen had not known anyone was inside the house. They had put out the fire, discovered Holley's body, and then called the police.

the hole in the floor seemed too big. Could an oil lamp have done that much damage?

Detectives sent Holley's body to the medical examiner for an **autopsy**. The autopsy should help answer the main question. Was Holley's death an accident, or murder?

Examining the Evidence

Was Marguerite Holley murdered?

When the **ME**'s report came in, detectives had their answer. The autopsy showed no soot or smoke in Holley's lungs. She hadn't breathed any smoke. She had been dead before the fire started. Holley had been strangled to death.

Police also ran lab tests on the bedroom floor. The tests found lighter fluid at the scene. That explained the damage to the floor. Someone had spread lighter fluid to start the fire.

The fire began here, in Holley's bedroom. Someone had used lighter fluid. That made the fire extremely hot. It also spread quickly and did a lot of damage.

Detectives now knew they were dealing with a homicide. But who would have reason to kill Marguerite Holley?

Police decided to bring in a criminal profiler.

The Profiler Steps In

Can Dayle Hinman figure out who might have killed Holley?

The Edgewater police called Dayle Hinman. Hinman often worked with Florida law enforcement on violent crime cases.

THE QUESTION Hinman started with an important question: Was the killer a stranger? Or did Holley know her attacker?

THE EVIDENCE After looking at crime scene photos, Hinman joined detectives at Holley's home.

The first thing she noted was the location of the house. It sat deep inside a quiet neighborhood, not on a main road.

Hinman then considered the timing of the murder. Holley died just before the fire started. The car had probably been taken right after the murder. That meant that the killer drove out of the neighborhood in broad daylight.

Dayle Hinman and another profiler, Wayne Porter, study a map that shows the area around Marguerite Holley's home.

Detectives showed Hinman the broken glass near the back door. The glass had fallen outside the door, not inside. The window had been broken from the inside.

THE CONCLUSION After her investigation, Hinman decided that Holley had known her murderer.

How did she arrive at her conclusion? First, the house was far off the beaten path. "It wasn't likely someone just happened to find her house," says Hinman. Second, the perp drove Holley's car through her neighborhood in broad daylight. He was probably someone who wouldn't look suspicious driving her car.

Hinman also reasoned that the killer had tried to cover his tracks. He probably broke the window to make the crime look like a robbery. And setting a fire in a home, Hinman says, is "almost always to try and cover up evidence."

WHO IS A PROFILER?
Profilers can be . . .

Police detectives who do profiles as part of their criminal investigation.

Professors of criminology or psychologists. Law enforcement agencies call them to help out on cases.

FBI agents who have trained at the FBI's Behavioral Sciences Unit. They might profile international terrorists, as well as **serial** killers.

Agents at state investigative agencies who have training in behavioral science. For example, the Tennessee Bureau of Investigation has profilers.

Employees of large corporations or security firms. They might profile computer hackers or Internet criminals.

Police Close In

Hinman's conclusions help investigators focus on a suspect. Did the handyman do it?

Thanks to Hinman, the Edgewater detectives knew where to search for a suspect. They interviewed Holley's friends. Did anyone have a motive for killing Holley?

Their questions soon led to a handyman named John Smith. Smith regularly did repair jobs around Holley's house. Friends said Holley thought Smith had been stealing from her.

Police tracked down people who knew Smith. Some of them claimed that he sometimes caused damage himself, then charged to repair it.

Investigators looked through Holley's records. Over the past six months, she had loaned Smith nearly $10,000.

The police got a warrant to search Smith's house. A police dog sniffed out a shirt in a pile of laundry. Tests later showed that the shirt contained lighter fluid. Investigators now had evidence to tie Smith to the fire.

DC Number:	617886
Name:	
Race:	WHITE
Sex:	MALE
Hair Color:	BROWN
Eye Color:	HAZEL
Height:	5'06"
Weight:	178
Birth Date:	
Initial Receipt Date:	09/02/1992
Current Facility:	GLADES C. I.
Current Classification Status:	NOT APPLICABLE
Current Custody:	CLOSE
Current Release Date:	SENTENCED TO LIFE

Hinman's investigation pointed the police to the handyman, John Smith. This document shows the criminal profiling information on this suspect.

Police arrested John Smith for the murder of Marguerite Holley. At his trial, the **prosecutor** described Smith's motive. He told the jury that Holley had grown tired of Smith's scams. Smith had killed her to prevent her from going to the police.

The jury believed the prosecutor. Smith was **convicted** and sentenced to life in prison.

The case left Hinman feeling satisfied with her work. "As a profiler, I look at a criminal's behavior for clues as to why he committed the crime," she says. "John Smith tried to hide his crime, and that's one of the things that led us to him."

Investigators examine evidence at a crime scene. Hinman's examination helped her create a profile of the suspect in the Holley case.

In this case, a profiler helped find the perp by examining the physical evidence. But how will a profiler deal with digital evidence? Find out in the next case.

The Case of the Mysterious Hacker

A university's computer network is under attack. Can a cyber-profiler find the hacker?

Note: The following case is true. Some places and names have been changed to protect people's privacy.

Montreal, Quebec, Canada
November 15, 1997
10:31 A.M.

Making the Grade

A university's computer is hacked, and grades are changed. Is a student to blame?

Concordia University sits in the heart of Montreal, Quebec, in Canada. More than 30,000 students go to school there. Like most college students, they care about their grades.

Grades matter, and the university has a computer system that keeps track of them. Locked away in the computer network are the records for 30,000 people.

In November 1997, someone unlocked that system.

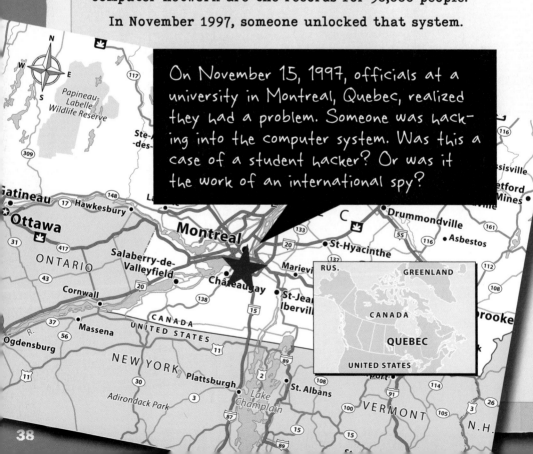

On November 15, 1997, officials at a university in Montreal, Quebec, realized they had a problem. Someone was hacking into the computer system. Was this a case of a student hacker? Or was it the work of an international spy?

On the morning of November 15, a professor noticed something wrong. Student grades in the computer files didn't match his records. He called the college's information technology (IT) staff. The IT staff logged into the system and found the problem. Someone was **hacking** into the system and changing grades.

The attack on the network wasn't just a prank. It was a crime under Canadian law. The college called the police. The police called computer **forensic** expert Dr. Marc Rogers.

The computer network at Concordia University has records on at least 30,000 people.

Nabbing an Amateur

Dr. Rogers follows the hacker's digital trail.

THE QUESTION Dr. Rogers started with a basic question. Was the hacker a student who simply wanted better grades? Or was this the work of a professional with a bigger goal in mind?

Then he got to work collecting evidence. The crime scene, however, wasn't on any map. This criminal's trail began in **cyberspace**.

THE EVIDENCE Rogers worked with the IT staff at the college. Together they figured out what Internet Service Provider (**ISP**) the hacker used.

Dr. Marc Rogers

talks about cyber-profiling.

Q How is digital crime scene analysis different from psychological crime scene analysis?

Dr. Rogers: Our investigations parallel psychological crime scene analysis. What are the **signature** behaviors, **characteristics**, or MO of the criminal? How does that help you narrow down the suspect pool? And how do you get them to talk? When you push the right buttons, these guys love to talk. The longest statements I've ever taken are from computer criminals!

Q What kinds of cases do you work on?

Dr. Rogers: Basic hackers, Internet **predators**. We also deal with attacks on corporate computer systems. One of the first things we do is determine if the attacker was an insider or an outsider.

Q Are computer criminals different from regular criminals?

Dr. Rogers: [To computer criminals,] it seems like a faceless corporation they're going after, not a person. There's a layer of **technology** between them and their victims. These guys wouldn't rob a bank or attack someone. But they have no problem doing these things virtually.

Next, Dr. Rogers contacted the ISP. Normally, ISPs refuse to give out information about their users. But this user had broken the ISP's rules by hacking into the school's computer. Police in Montreal presented their case to a judge. The judge ordered the ISP to let Dr. Rogers onto their network.

Dr. Marc Rogers (right) often gives advice to people in law enforcement. Here, he's working with Dale Lloyd of the Indiana State Police.

Dr. Rogers drove to the offices of the ISP. He examined the **servers**. He followed the hacker's trail in computer records. The hacker had used well-known computer tools to unlock the university's system. This was no skilled pro, Rogers decided. A professional would have written his own computer code. The hacker was most likely a student.

Dr. Rogers got the user's account information from the ISP. The police went to the hacker's home. The suspect was a student, and he confessed to hacking the university's system. He was expelled from school.

Case closed? Not quite.

A System Under Attack

The investigation goes further. Is there a professional hacker involved?

While Dr. Rogers was examining the ISP's servers, he discovered something suspicious. At certain times, the servers slowed down. After about an hour, they sped up again. Someone was running programs behind the server's normal activity.

This new activity didn't fit the MO of the student hacker. The programs were too complex. Someone else was at work here. At special times they logged in and took over the ISP. But why?

Was this hacker using the ISP to attack a larger computer system? If so, he could be a lot more dangerous than a student who wanted better grades.

Profile of a Pro

A second hacker is discovered—along with an international plot.

Dr. Rogers shifted his investigation to search for the new hacker.

At first, Rogers was confused by the system slowdowns. They happened regularly, always in the middle of the day. Rogers used his tracking software to trace the hacker.

The activity was coming from the former country of Yugoslavia. That explained the timing of the slowdowns. "The hacker was logging on in what was the middle of the night for him," says Dr. Rogers.

So the hacker worked in secret in the middle of the night. Why? What was the target? The answer was startling. The hacker was scanning the computers of the U.S. military.

Dr. Rogers now knew what he was dealing with. This was the work of a professional criminal or cyber-terrorist. It was time to hand the case over to the government.

CRIMINAL HACKERS
What kinds of people commit computer crimes?

Not all computer criminals are alike. But they do tend to fit a pattern. Here's Dr. Rogers's profile of a typical cyber-criminal.

- Most computer criminals are male.
- They aren't necessarily loners.
- They aren't necessarily smarter than other criminals.
- In general, computer criminals don't realize what they're doing is wrong. They don't always realize they're committing a crime.

The Feds Take Over

The discovery of a possible terrorist grabs the government's attention.

Dr. Rogers may have identified a major spying operation. He used plenty of high-tech tools to do it. But he still needed a profiler's basic skills.

Rogers understood the MOs of various types of hackers. That knowledge helped him tell the difference between a college student and an international hacker. Without it, the problem with the servers might have gone unexplained. Some might have thought it was the student hacker. Others would have looked for a technical problem.

The country of Yugoslavia was formed in 1945. It started to break into different countries in the 1990s. Now, this area includes the countries of Bosnia and Herzegovina, Croatia, Montenegro, Republic of Macedonia, Serbia, and Slovenia.

Once Rogers had profiled the hacker, he was done with the case. Federal officials in Canada and the U.S. took over. It became a top-secret anti-terrorism investigation. Dr. Rogers never learned the outcome of the case.

FORENSIC DOWNLOAD

Here's your guide to the past, present, and future of criminal profiling.

In this section:

▶ how a BEHAVIOR PROFILE was created for Adolf Hitler;

▶ why CRIMINAL PROFILING is making headlines;

▶ tools profilers use to do their RESEARCH;

▶ whether criminal profiling might be in YOUR FUTURE.

1888 First Modern Criminal Profile

Someone is brutally murdering women in London. Police surgeon Dr. Thomas Bond performs an autopsy on the latest victim, Mary Kelly. Dr. Bond describes the kind of person who might have committed the murders. For example, he claims that the killer has some medical knowledge.

In the process, Dr. Bond creates the first modern "profile." His subject? One of history's most famous killers—Jack the Ripper! (This murderer may have written the letter to the left.)

Key Dates in Profiling

How did criminal profiling become a valuable part of police work?

Early 1940s Profiling at War

During World War II, German dictator Adolf Hitler is terrorizing the world. U.S. military leaders want to know more about him. They ask psychiatrist Walter Langer to create a profile of Hitler. Langer predicts that Hitler will kill himself rather than be captured. That prediction comes true.

1970 Setting Profiling Standards

FBI agent Howard Teten creates his first profile. Teten later develops the applied criminology course at the FBI National Academy. His work leads to the FBI's Behavioral Sciences Unit (BSU). The BSU trains profilers.

1978–83 Researching Serial Killers

FBI **agents** conduct a study of serial killers. They interview jailed murderers to see what they have in common. The researchers divide killers into two categories—organized and disorganized. This method is still used by some FBI profilers.

1981 Profiling Hits the Big Time

Thomas Harris publishes *Red Dragon*. The book introduces serial killer Hannibal Lecter. Harris follows *Red Dragon* with *The Silence of the Lambs* in 1988. The two books make the FBI's Behavioral Sciences Unit famous.

2002 Anthrax Attacker Stumps Profilers

Deadly anthrax spores are sent in the mail to public figures. FBI profilers decide that the attacks are the work of a single scientist. Six years later, the criminal has not been caught. The FBI profile is questioned. Some think the attacks were the work of terrorists.

2006 An Ever-Changing Field

Criminal profiling is growing and changing. As research on criminal activity grows, profilers get more scientific. They work with new techniques. Cyber-profilers, like Dr. Marc Rogers, use computer software to track criminals. So do geographic profilers. They use crime data to figure out where a criminal lives.

See Case #3: The Case of the Mysterious Hacker.

In the News

Criminal profiling is front-page news.

Real Profiler in the Spotlight!

NEW YORK CITY—July 15, 2002

Broadcasting and Cable magazine reports that Court TV is adding a new reality show to their lineup. The show is called *Body of Evidence*. It will feature real-life profiler Dayle Hinman, one of the few women in the profession.

Hinman worked for 26 years in Florida's Department of Law Enforcement. She helped put hundreds of criminals behind bars. In *Body of Evidence*, Hinman re-creates the details of her most fascinating cases.

Above: Profiler Dayle Hinman has her own TV show about criminal profiling. It's called Body of Evidence. Left: Hinman gets ready for the next shot on the set of her show.

Ted Kaczynski had bombed universities and airlines since 1978. He was arrested in 1996. Here, he's being led to the courthouse in Helena, Montana, on April 4.

FBI Ignores Accurate Profile!

November 17, 1997

Bill Tafoya got it right. The FBI profiler tracked the Unabomber in 1993. The Unabomber had been sending bombs to universities and airlines since 1978.

Tafoya and fellow agent Mary Ellen O'Toole predicted that the bomber was in his early 50s. They thought he was well educated and hated technology.

The FBI ignored the profile. Instead, they looked for a younger man who worked in the airplane industry. They finally arrested Ted Kaczynski on April 3, 1996. He was 53, had a PhD, and hated technology.

Kaczynski lived in this one-room cabin in Lincoln, Montana, for almost 25 years.

Body of Evidence

Have a look at the documents, tools, and software used by criminal profilers.

CRIME SCENE PHOTOS AND POLICE REPORTS

Many criminal profilers work from crime scene photos rather than going to the crime scene with the police. They can tell a lot from the position of a body, wounds on a body, things left behind at a scene, how victim was attacked, and so on.

[Forensic Fact]

Geographical profiling takes into account known movement patterns. For example, right-handed criminals escaping in a hurry flee to the left. They toss their weapons to the right. When lost, men tend to go downhill. Women tend to go uphill.

LAB REPORTS

Profilers must be able to read and understand lab reports by medical examiners, DNA specialists, and other forensic scientists. They gain important information from these reports, such as the cause of death and location of the wounds.

reports on insects found on corpse

forensic dental forms

FORENSIC ENTOMOLOGY DATA FORM

CASE NUMBER: _____

E: _____   AGENCY: _____

forest_____ field_____ pasture_____ brush_____ roadside_
barren area_____ closed building_____ open building_____
other_____
uburban: closed building_____ open building_____
vacant lot_____ pavement_____ trash container_____
other_____
habitat: pond_____ lake_____ creek_____ small river___
large river_____ irrigation canal_____ ditch_____ gulf___
swampy area_____ drainage ditch_____ salt water_____
fresh water_____ brackish water_____
other_____
e: Open air_____ burial/depth_____
clothing entire_____ partial_____ nude_____
portion of body clothed_____
description of clothing_____
type of debris on body_____
decomposition: fresh_____ bloat_____ active decay_____
advanced decay_____ skeletonization_____ saponification___
mummification_____ dismemberment_____
other: _____
ngers: _____
c injury sites: (Comment or draw below)

: ambient:_____ ambient (1ft) _____ body surface_____
und surface_____ under-body interface_____ maggot mass_
ter temp, if aquatic_____ enclosed structure_____ AC/Heat- o
ling fan- on/off_____ soil temperature- 10cm_____ 20cm___
d samples _____ Number of live samples_____
emperatures periodically each day at the site for 3-5 days after bod
COPYRIGHT DR. J. H. BYRD ©1998-2000

CAPMI SYMBOLS

PRIMARY CODES		SECONDARY CODES	
C	CROWN	A	ANOMALY, ROOT TIP. ANY PATHOLOGY
D	DISTAL	B	PRIMARY TOOTH
F	FACIAL	G	GOLD, CAST METAL.
L	LINGUAL		STAINLESS STEEL
M	MESIAL	N	NON-METÁLLIC
O	OCCLUSAL/INCISAL		RESTORATION
U	UNERUPTED	P	PONTIC
V	VIRGIN TOOTH	R	ROOT CANAL FILLING
X	MISSING TOOTH	S	SILVER AMALGAM
/	JAW FRAGMENT	T	REMOVABLE PROS
	MISSING,	Z	CARIES
	NONRECOGNIZABLE,		
	FRACTURED CROWN,		
	TRAUMATIC AVULSION		

X-Ray Type: _____   Date: _____
X-Ray Type: _____   Date: _____
X-Ray Type: _____   Date: _____
Examiners: _____

ANOMALY, ROOT TIP,
ANY PATHOLOGY
RIMARY TOOTH
OLD, CAST METAL.
AINLESS STEEL
N-METALLIC
TORATION
NTIC
T CANAL FILLING
ER AMALGAM
OVABLE PROS
ES

21.
22.
23.
24.
25.
26.
27.
28.
29.
30.
31.
32.

ay Type: _____   Date: _____
X-Ray Type: _____   Date: _____
Examiners: _____   Date: _____

REMARKS

RESEARCH

Profilers also read books, articles, and research by psychologists and other profilers. They might compare cases they're working on to similar cases that have been solved by other profilers. They keep up-to-date on the latest psychological research and developments in forensic science.

COMPUTERS

Profilers may also use these tools.

geographical profiling software: used to map locations of crimes to predict where the perp lives.

cyber-profiling software: used to track down the location of the computer used by a hacker or an Internet predator.

VICAP: a database with information about violent crimes, especially murder. VICAP stands for *Violent Criminal Apprehension Program*.

CODIS: the FBI's DNA database. It contains DNA samples of more than 300,000 convicted criminals. CODIS stands for *Combined DNA Index System*.

AFIS: That's a computer database where police can store the prints of arrested suspects. AFIS stands for *Automated Fingerprint Identification System*.

NETWORKING

Profilers often work with other profilers, psychologists, and police **experts**. Many develop ongoing relationships with these professionals and ask their opinions on cases.

"I'm part of a group of 150 forensic scientists who use a secure Web site to share information," says profiler Dayle Hinman. "These are profilers, psychologists, and medical examiners from all over the world.

"If I want the opinion of other profilers, I can go to this Web site. I can give the group information on a case. They can tell me what they think. I may not have all the answers, but I know who to ask!"

Help Wanted: Criminal Profiler

Are you interested in investigating criminal profiling?
Here's more information about the field.

Q&A: DAYLE HINMAN
DR. MARC ROGERS
DR. MAURICE GODWIN

Criminal profiler Dayle Hinman is the star of the truTV series *Body of Evidence: From the Case Files of Dayle Hinman*.

Q How did you get into this field?

Rogers: I had a degree in criminology and psychology, and then I became a law enforcement officer. I was working on my PhD in forensic psychology. I became interested in understanding why people commit criminal acts using technology. So all my interests seemed to meld together.

Hinman: I was career law enforcement. I received a fellowship at the FBI's Behavioral Science Unit. I wanted to be the person out there trying to find out what happened and why. [I didn't want to be] the secretary who typed the report about it!

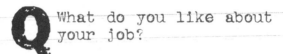

Q What do you like about your job?

Hinman: I like everything about it. You would expect that my job would be depressing, but it's not. You do have to deal with a lot of people who are dead or dying. But I like being able to focus an investigation on the type of person who committed a crime. I like being part of the team that figures out who did it.

Godwin: A lot of what I like is the mystery. It appeals to my curiosity. It's a challenge to find out who did it.

Q What skills come in handy for a profiler?

Godwin: The first thing you need is curiosity—to search and find the unknown. You also need logic. They even teach logic courses at universities.

Hinman: I see the ability to observe and the ability to listen as important attributes. So few people go to a crime scene and actually see what's there. You have to notice all the details. And you need to be someone who takes the job seriously and works hard.

Cyber-profiler Dr. Marc Rogers is a professor of cyber-forensics at Purdue University in Indiana.

Q What advice do you have for young people interested in this field?

Godwin: You must have a solid background in psychology. And for geographical profiling, statistics courses are good. It also helps to have courses in criminal investigation and forensic science. And once you get your degree, join professional organizations and go to conferences and such. Most profilers are **consultants**, so it's good to get your name out there.

Hinman: I think it helps to have law enforcement experience.

Rogers: I'm starting to see lots more students in this field. Young people are not as freaked out by technology as the older behavioral scientists might have been. I think if you're interested in computers and criminology, this is a growing field for you.

THE STATS

Day Job

Many criminal profilers are practicing psychologists. Others are specially trained police officers. Still others are FBI agents. Even professors of criminology are called on to consult when they're needed.

Money

Police officers average between $34,000 and $56,000 a year. Psychologists average between $41,000 and $65,000 a year. FBI agents start at $48,000 a year.

Education

Criminal profilers must finish four years of college. FBI agents must finish four years of college and train to become an FBI agent. They must join the FBI's Behavioral Sciences Unit.

Dr. Maurice Godwin develops psychological profiles of criminals. He also creates geographical profiles to show where suspects probably live.

DO YOU HAVE WHAT IT TAKES?

Take this totally unscientific quiz to find out if criminal profiling might be a good career for you.

1 Do you have good instincts about people?
a) Yes, I can usually tell what someone is like.
b) Sometimes, but I've made some major mistakes.
c) I like everyone, so I often am disappointed in people.

2 Are you curious and logical?
a) Yes, I'm always asking questions and I come up with pretty good conclusions.
b) I'm a little curious about some things.
c) Not really. I tend to look at situations and jump to conclusions.

3 Would you say you work well with others?
a) Yes, I'm most creative when I'm part of a group.
b) Most of the time.
c) I'm a loner. People often get on my nerves!

4 How do you think you respond to news about violent and disturbing crimes?
a) It upsets me, but I mostly just hope the perp is caught.
b) Sometimes I really just can't listen.
c) Don't tell me about that kind of stuff. I can't take it!

5 Do you enjoy studying behavior and understanding why people do what they do?
a) Yes, that's so cool.
b) Sometimes.
c) No, that's pretty boring.

YOUR SCORE

Give yourself 3 points for every "**a**" you chose.

Give yourself 2 points for every "**b**" you chose.

Give yourself 1 point for every "**c**" you chose.

If you got **13–15 points**, you'd probably be a good criminal profiler.

If you got **10–12 points**, you might be a good criminal profiler.

If you got **5–9 points**, you might want to look at another career!

INCHES
1
2
3
4
5
6
7
8
9
10

HOW TO GET STARTED...NOW!

It's never too early to start working toward your goals.

GET AN EDUCATION

▶ Focus on behavior science classes (like psychology or sociology) and computer science.

▶ Start thinking about college. Look for ones with good forensic science or computer forensic programs.

▶ Read the newspaper. Keep up with what's going on in your community.

▶ Read anything you can find about criminal profiling and psychology.

▶ See the books and Web sites in the Resources section on pages 108–112.

▶ Graduate from high school!

NETWORK!

Find out about forensic groups in your area. See if you can find a local criminal profiler who might be willing to give you advice.

GET AN INTERNSHIP

Look for an internship with a local law enforcement agency. Look for an internship at a local medical examiner's office.

LEARN ABOUT OTHER JOBS IN THE FIELD

Employees of large corporations or security firms sometimes profile hackers or Internet criminals.

A body is found. It shows no signs of violence. Police can't find fingerprints or a murder weapon. What happened?

FORENSIC 411

The victim may have been poisoned. If so, the body still holds traces of the poison. What was it? Where did it come from? Finding out is a job for a forensic toxicologist.

In this section:

- ▶ how forensic TOXICOLOGISTS really talk;
- ▶ some HIDDEN CLUES toxicologists look for in a victim's body;
- ▶ who else is working at the CRIME SCENE.

Toxic Talk

Forensic toxicologists have their own way of speaking. Find out what their **vocabulary** means.

toxicology
(TOK-sik-ahl-uh-jee) the science of finding, treating, and studying poisons. Toxicologists study how poisons affect plants, animals, the environment, and humans.

"There's no obvious cause of death. Make sure you get toxicology results on the body."

"Toxic" has to do with poison. "Ology" means "the study of."

"Did the victim have any strange symptoms before she passed out?"

symptoms
(SIMP-tums) signs of an illness or some physical problem

"I'm starting to suspect that she might have been accidentally poisoned."

poisoned
(POY-zuhnd) taken a substance that causes injury, illness, or death

"Test for every drug you can think of. She took something toxic, and I want to know what it was."

drug
(druhg) a product or chemical that can change the way the body works. Drugs from a doctor can be used to treat illnesses.

toxic
(TOK-sik) poisonous

"This might not be murder. They found deadly toxins in a waste dump not far from here."

toxin
(TOK-sihn) any substance that can kill cells or cause injury or death; a poison

Say What?

Here's some other lingo a forensic toxicologist might use on the job.

acute
(uh-KYOOT) describing a poisoning that is quick and intense

*"The victim was fine yesterday. This must be a case of **acute** poisoning."*

chain of custody
(chayn uhv KUH-stuh-dee) the list of people who handle evidence, in the order in which they handle it. In court, lawyers can attack toxicology tests if evidence is not handled properly.

*"This is an important case. Make sure there are no mistakes on the **chain of custody** for the blood sample."*

chronic
(KRAH-nik) describing a poisoning that happens over time in small doses

*"This was a case of **chronic** poisoning. The victim had symptoms for months before she died."*

HAIR: In a living person, hair stores toxins much longer than blood or urine. That helps **forensic** toxicologists test for drugs and other toxins.

LUNGS: If a toxin is in gas form, it will probably leave traces in a **victim's** lungs.

STOMACH: Toxicologists look at the stomach to find out how much of a drug was digested before death. The results can help them figure out when a drug was taken.

KIDNEYS: Kidneys filter waste—including poisons—out of the blood. They turn the waste into urine so the body can get rid of it. Toxicologists test urine for toxins.

STOMACH, INTESTINES, LIVER: Gulp! Any drug that's been swallowed travels from the stomach to the intestines and the liver.

BLOOD: Blood is a toxicologist's best friend. Nearly every drug can be found in the blood. Blood tests can show how much of a toxin was taken and how it affected the body.

MUSCLES: Some drugs enter the body through a needle. Those drugs may go directly into a muscle. Toxicologists test muscles around the needle mark to find out what kind of drug is present.

EYES: The liquid in your eyeballs is called *vitreous humor*. Many **chemicals** found in the blood end up here. It takes about two hours for a poison to travel from your blood to your vitreous humor. Testing the liquid can help determine the time of death.

Body of Evidence

LIVER: The liver filters toxins from the blood. Then it turns the toxins into a liquid called **bile**. Testing the liver and the bile can show when a poison was taken. It can tell toxicologists if a poisoning was acute or chronic.

Poisons end up in different places in the human body. Here's where toxicologists look for signs of poisoning.

INSECTS: Insects that feed off of a dead body take in chemicals from the person's body. Toxicologists sometimes test these bugs to look for **evidence** of drugs in a victim.

TISSUES: Drugs that are injected with a needle may not show up in the stomach or liver. They can often be found in tissues almost anywhere else in the body.

63

The Forensic Team

Forensic toxicologists work as part of a team. Here's a look at some of the experts who help solve the crimes.

Forensic Entomologists

They study the insects on or near a body. They can also figure out if there are poisons in bugs found on the victim's body.

First Responder Police Officers/Detectives

They are often the ones to find, collect, and transport the evidence. They take photos and give the forensic toxicologist the crime scene data.

FORENSIC PATHOLOGISTS/ MEDICAL EXAMINERS

They're medical doctors who investigate suspicious deaths. They try to find out when and how someone died. They often direct other members of the team.

Forensic Toxicologists

They test victims for drugs, alcohol, and/ or poison.

Forensic Anthropologists

They're called in to identify victims by studying bones.

Lawyers

They argue cases in court. They either defend someone accused of a crime, or they try to prove that the suspect is guilty.

Fingerprint Examiners

They find, photograph, and collect fingerprints at the scene. Then they compare them to prints they have on record.

Forensic Dentists

They identify victims and criminals by their teeth or bitemarks.

TRUE-LIFE CASE FILES!

24 hours a day, 7 days a week, 365 days a year, forensic toxicologists are solving mysteries.

In this section:

- ▶ how a few strange green specks helped FBI AGENTS put a poisoner in jail;

- ▶ whether a presidential candidate was REALLY POISONED;

- ▶ why TOXICOLOGISTS think a famous emperor may not have died of natural causes.

24/7 Science Behind the Scenes

the Scenes

Here's how forensic toxicologists get the job done.

What does it take to solve a crime? Good forensic toxicologists don't just make guesses. They're scientists. They follow a step-by-step process.

As you read the case studies, you can follow along with these scientists. Keep an eye out for the icons below. They'll clue you in to each step along the way.

THE QUESTION
(?) At the beginning of a case, toxicologists *identify one or two main questions* they have to answer.

THE EVIDENCE
(?) The next step is to *gather and analyze evidence*. Toxicologists collect blood or tissue samples. They gather as much evidence as they can. Then they test it to see what they can conclude.

THE CONCLUSION
(!) Finally, toxicologists *study the test results to reach a conclusion*. If they've done their job well, their evidence might help crack the case.

The Case of the Deadly Drug

Two people are dead after taking a common pain medicine. Who could have poisoned the pills?

"Something's Wrong with Her!"

A healthy mom drops dead in the bathroom. What could have killed her?

The 911 call came at 6:43 A.M. on June 11, 1986. Fifteen-year-old Hayley Snow had trouble getting the words out. "I think my mother fell while I was in the shower. . . . She's breathing and everything, but something's wrong with her."

In the bathroom at their home in Auburn, Washington, Sue Snow lay on the floor. Her eyes were open, staring at the wall. Yet she didn't seem to be **conscious**. She couldn't talk to Hayley, and she was gasping for air.

Emergency medical technicians arrived while Hayley was still on the phone. Sue Snow was taken by helicopter to Harborview Medical Center in Seattle. She died there several hours later.

Doctors at Harborview couldn't explain what happened. At 40, Sue Snow was in perfect health. How could she have died so suddenly?

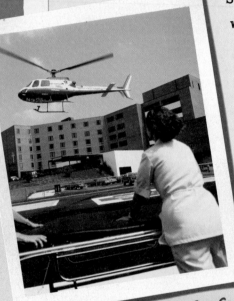

After she collapsed, Sue Snow was rushed by helicopter to Harborview Medical Center in Seattle. But it was too late.

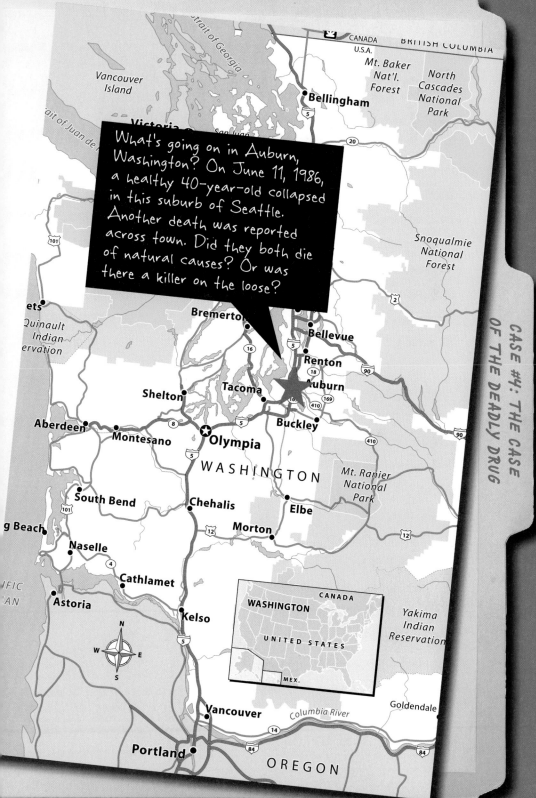

What's going on in Auburn, Washington? On June 11, 1986, a healthy 40-year-old collapsed in this suburb of Seattle. Another death was reported across town. Did they both die of natural causes? Or was there a killer on the loose?

The Scent of Almonds

It's time for an autopsy and drug tests. Was Sue Snow poisoned?

Doctors ordered an **autopsy** for Sue Snow. Dr. Corinne Fligner, the assistant **ME**, or medical examiner, went to work. Her assistant, Janet Miller, made the first incision. A faint but clear scent rose from the body: almonds. Miller knew right away what it was. "I smell **cyanide**," she told Fligner.

It turned out that Miller was right. Fligner sent a sample of Snow's blood to the toxicology lab. On June 16, the tests came back positive. Most likely, Snow had been murdered.

The case began to sound familiar to police. In 1982, a killer in the Chicago area secretly slipped cyanide into Tylenol capsules. Seven people died after taking the

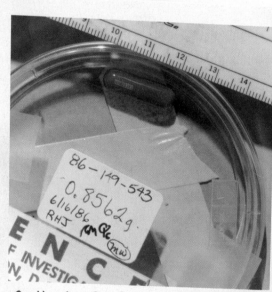

On the day Sue Snow died, the police collected all the pills from her home. This is just one of the pills that was collected as evidence and sent for testing.

70

A KILLER POISON
How cyanide does its dirty work.

Anyone who's read detective novels knows about cyanide. As a powder, it has very little smell or taste. A tiny pinch can be fatal. It can kill in minutes.

Despite how deadly it is, cyanide isn't hard to buy. Photographers use it to develop film. Jewelry makers use it in metalworking. It's found in insect poisons and blue dyes. You can even find it in certain foods. Apricot pits, almonds, lima beans, and spinach have cyanide in them. But the amounts are small enough to be harmless.

Doctors find the symptoms hard to identify. The one sign is a faint smell of bitter almonds that only some people can smell.

Cyanide put Sue Snow in a **coma** in less than an hour. It kills by making cells unable to use oxygen. It left Snow gasping for air to get more oxygen into her body.

poisoned pills. According to Snow's daughter, Snow had taken two Excedrin pain relievers half an hour before she died. Was it possible that a copycat killer was poisoning Excedrin capsules?

Just after lunch, police officers arrived at Sue Snow's house. Her husband agreed to allow a search. Police took every pill bottle they could find, including an opened bottle of Excedrin. They sent the pills to a lab for testing.

Just after 8 P.M., the results came in. Nine of the 56 capsules had cyanide in them.

Killer on the Loose

The FBI takes over—and the body count goes up to two.

On June 17, the **FBI** took over Sue Snow's murder case. Special Agent Jack Cusack was ordered to lead the investigation. By now, the death was big news. Drug companies offered a reward for information about the killer.

Dozens of FBI agents went to drugstores in the Seattle area. They collected thousands of Excedrin bottles. Right away, tests found a second poisoned bottle.

That day, a strange call led local police to bottles three and four. The caller was a 42-year-old woman named Stella Nickell.

Nickell told police that her husband, Bruce, had died 12 days earlier. The ME had said that the cause was lung disease. But Stella Nickell told police that her husband had taken four Excedrin just before he died. She thought he must have been poisoned. She had even called the ME's office three times to question their decision.

Nickell handed over two Excedrin bottles. She had bought them at two different stores. In two days, the

Bristol-Myers is the company that made Excedrin. Executives there ordered stores around the country to take all the bottles off their shelves.

test results were in. Between the bottles, six pills contained cyanide.

On June 24, agents found a fifth poisoned bottle in a local drugstore.

EVIDENCE

The police collected all the Excedrin from Stella Nickell's house. Had her husband also died from poisoned pills?

Mystery Specks

The FBI toxicology lab examines the pills. A few tiny green specks might hold a clue.

So far, Cusack had one important piece of physical evidence: the poisoned pills. Agents carefully packed up the bottles. They shipped them to the FBI lab in Washington, D.C.

THE QUESTION A young chemist named Roger Martz took charge of the bottles. Could he find out where the poison came from?

Martz's main job was to "fingerprint" the poison. Only three U.S. companies made cyanide. Each version had a different chemical makeup, or fingerprint. If Martz could figure out who made the cyanide, it might pinpoint where the killer bought it.

Martz examined the capsules.

THE EVIDENCE He found an average of 700 mg of cyanide in each. A dose of 70 mg will kill the average adult. He also found tiny green specks in nearly all of the poisoned capsules.

Chemicals in the specks had mixed with the cyanide. That ruined Martz's attempts to fingerprint the poison.

But did the specks hold an even more important clue?

Martz tested the specks. He found three chemicals normally used to kill algae in fish tanks. The killer, he decided, could have mixed the cyanide in a container used to hold the algae killer. Martz measured the exact amount of each chemical. That led him to the exact brand of algae killer.

THE CONCLUSION The murderer, Martz decided, probably used a product called Algae Destroyer.

A Fish Story

The evidence piles up. Is Stella Nickell lying?

Back in Seattle, Special Agent Cusack was beginning to wonder about Stella Nickell. First of all, Nickell had not one, but two, of the poisoned bottles. The FBI had collected and tested 15,000 bottles in all. Five of them had cyanide. And Stella Nickell was unlucky enough to buy two of them? That seemed nearly impossible.

Cusack looked into Nickell's background. Just before her husband's death, the couple had been running out of money. Stella Nickell had three insurance policies on her husband's life. Two

Police began to wonder if Stella Nickell had played a part in the poisoning death of her husband, Bruce.

had just been bought in 1985. The third paid an extra $105,000 if Bruce Nickell died accidentally. Cyanide poisoning was an accidental death.

Finally, Martz's test results reached Seattle. The investigator who first went to the Nickell's house remembered an important detail. Stella Nickell had a fish tank.

Cusack sent an agent to pet stores in the area with pictures of Stella Nickell. On August

Algae is the slimy green stuff that grows in fish tanks. Many fish owners use Algae Destroyer to get rid of it. Was Stella Nickell one of them?

25, he found a clerk who remembered her. And yes, he said, Nickell used Algae Destroyer.

The Final Piece

A daughter tells a tale of murder.

By the fall, Cusack thought he had found his killer. Stella Nickell came in for questioning. She said she had never bought Algae Destroyer. She also claimed she had only one insurance policy.

In December she came back to take a lie-detector test. She failed.

However, lie-detector tests cannot be used in court. So Cusack needed solid evidence. Then, in January,

Nickell's 27-year-old daughter, Cindy Hamilton, called. She said her mother had talked for years about wanting to kill her husband. Stella Nickell had even researched poisons at the library.

Cusack sent an agent to the local library. The FBI fingerprinting lab found 84 of Stella Nickel's prints on a book about poisons. The most handled pages were the ones on cyanide.

Stella Nickell had checked out two books with information about poisons. Agents found her fingerprints on one of them.

On December 9, 1987, Jack Cusack and Ron Nichols drove to Stella Nickell's home. They arrested her for the murder of her husband, Bruce Nickell.

In April 1988, Stella went on trial for the deaths of Sue Snow and Bruce Nickell. The prosecutor called her an "icy human being without social or moral conscience." On May 9, 1988, a **jury** found her guilty. The judge sentenced her to 99 years in jail.

All the while, Nickell has claimed she is innocent. Her daughter, Cindy, collected $250,000 in reward money from the drug companies. Nickell said Cindy lied in order to get the money. Since 1988, Stella Nickell has filed for a new trial three times. Three times her appeals have been rejected.

In the next case, find out about a poisoning that made the whole world watch.

The Case of the Poisoned Politician

September 6, 2004
Kiev, in Ukraine
3:30 A.M.

One night, Viktor Yushchenko is battling for the presidency of Ukraine. The next day, he is fighting for his life.

Ukraine won its independence from Russia in 1991. Ukranians finally had the right to hold free elections. But in the fall of 2004, that right seemed to be in danger. A presidential candidate said that he had been poisoned by his opponents!

Deadly Dinner Date

After a dinner with some political rivals, Viktor Yushchenko becomes violently ill.

On September 5, 2004, Viktor Yushchenko had an important dinner date. He hoped to become the next president of Ukraine. He was popular with the people. But his opponent had the support of the government. And in Ukraine, the government was a powerful force. It controlled the country's newspapers and TV stations. It also controlled the secret police.

The head of the secret police was hosting Yushchenko that night. They sat down to dinner at 10 P.M. with two other men. Yuschenko's bodyguards stayed behind. The men talked about Ukraine's future. They discussed Yuschenko's safety. The candidate had received death threats recently. He wanted protection from the secret police.

While they talked, the men ate crayfish and salad. They drank beer and vodka.

In 2004, Viktor Yushchenko announced that he would run for president. His main opponent was Viktor Yanukovych. Yushchenko was very popular, but Yanukovych was backed by the government.

They ended their meeting with an after-dinner drink.

At about 3:30 A.M., Yushchenko drove home. In the car, his head began to pound with pain. At home, he kissed his wife. She noticed a bitter, metallic taste on his lips. Within an hour, Yushchenko started to vomit.

Hours later, Yushchenko was rushed to the hospital. The night before, he was planning to become the next president of Ukraine. Now, he was close to death.

Written on His Face

Was Yushchenko poisoned? Or just the victim of a bad meal?

Doctors in Ukraine had no idea what was wrong with Yushchenko. They flew him to a hospital in Austria. He arrived in terrible pain. He had a crippling backache. His stomach was lined with sores. His pancreas, which creates the juices to help digest food, was swollen.

The Austrian doctors had never seen an illness like Yushchenko's. They decided the candidate's illness had been caused by chemicals not found in food.

That was all the information Yushchenko needed. He was furious. Doctors tried to keep him in the hospital. He refused. He had a campaign to run, he said. A week later, Yushchenko was back in Ukraine.

In three days, he appeared in parliament. He accused his opponents of poisoning him. "You know very well who the killer is," he said. "The killer is the government."

Yushchenko's opponents fought back. They said Yushchenko had simply had too much to drink. Others claimed he got sick from eating spoiled fish.

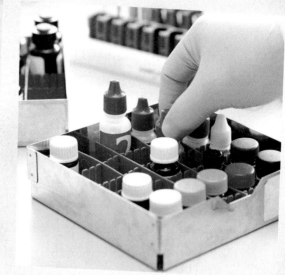

By this time, Yushchenko looked terrible. His face was swollen and pale. His cheeks were covered with a rash.

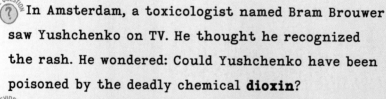
Many poisons can be found in the blood, and these chemicals are used to find them. After a toxicologist saw Yushchenko on TV, Yushchenko's blood was checked for poisons.

THE QUESTION ? In Amsterdam, a toxicologist named Bram Brouwer saw Yushchenko on TV. He thought he recognized the rash. He wondered: Could Yushchenko have been poisoned by the deadly chemical **dioxin**?

THE EVIDENCE ? Brouwer called the hospital in Austria. He asked for a sample of Yushchenko's blood.

Down But Not Defeated

Back from the dead, can Yushchenko win the presidency?

Yushchenko traveled his country in pain. He gave speeches and attacked his opponent. Ukraine, he said, was not yet a free country. The government was corrupt. It controlled the media. It had even tried to steal the election by murdering a candidate.

Ukranians responded with their support. Voters sent cards and letters to Yushchenko. Thousands prayed for his recovery.

But the election ended without a clear decision. It was held on October 31. Yushchenko won 39.9 percent of the vote. His opponent, Viktor Yanukovych, won 39.3 percent. The other 20 percent of voters chose minor candidates. No candidate won the 50 percent needed to make him president.

On November 21, voters went back to the polls. This time, they had to choose between Yushchenko and Yanukovych.

Yushchenko waited eagerly for the results. He was recovering but still in pain. His face still looked terribly deformed.

News organizations held exit polls. As Ukranians left the polling places, they were asked whom they voted for. The results showed Yushchenko in the lead. One poll said he was winning by 11 percent.

By December 2006, Yushchenko's face had been terribly damaged by the dioxin poisoning.

Viktor Yanukovych was Yushchenko's opponent in the 2004 election. He was declared the winner of one of the first elections.

But when the vote was finally counted, the results looked much different. The official result: Yanukovych was the winner by 3 percent.

The Orange Revolution

Ukranians march in the streets to protest the election.

After the vote, Yushchenko's supporters were furious. How could the official results be so different from the exit polls? Yushchenko insisted that the government had cheated. He refused to accept the results.

A day after the election, thousands of people filled the streets. They chanted Yushchenko's name. They waved orange flags in honor of Yushchenko's campaign color. They demanded that he be named president. Yushchenko urged them on.

As days passed, the protests grew larger. People set up tents in the streets of Kiev, the country's capital. Riot police with shields and helmets came out to meet

In December 2004, people gathered in Independence Square in Kiev to protest what they believed was an unfair election. Because Yushchenko's party used the color orange, these protests became known as the Orange Revolution.

them. Huge crowds moved to take over government buildings. The police did little to stop them.

Finally, the country's supreme court ruled the election unfair. Both sides agreed on a new election for December 26.

On December 8, protesters began to leave the streets. The "Orange Revolution" was over. Yushchenko appeared before a huge crowd. "During these 17 days, we have gotten a new country," he said.

Yushchenko turned his attention to the election. He was confident now. A new piece of news made him sure to win.

On December 11, Bram Brouwer, the Dutch toxicologist, announced the results of his tests. He said that Yushchenko had been poisoned by dioxin. The level of poison in his blood was 1,000 times higher than normal.

On December 26, Yushchenko won the election with 52 percent of the vote.

Yushchenko celebrates his victory on December 26, 2004.

WHAT IS DIOXIN?
This deadly chemical is widespread.

Don't look now! There's dioxin in your food. This deadly chemical comes from factories that use chlorine. It also comes from the manufacturing of plastics, paper, and **pesticides**.

Dioxin makes its way into the environment. It seeps into the soil. It washes into rivers. It eventually reaches animals—including you. Nearly every person has low levels of dioxin in the body.

Dioxin can be dangerous over long periods of time. It can cause cancer or birth defects. It builds up in body fat. It can stay in your body for 35 years. In the short term, high levels can cause skin rashes and digestion problems.

Case Closed?

The president takes office while the investigation continues. Was Yushchenko really poisoned?

Was Yushchenko really poisoned? A top official for Yushchenko claims the dioxin in his blood was a chemical called T-2. The Russians developed this chemical as a weapon during the Cold War. The head of Russia, Vladimir Putin, supported Yushchenko's opponent. Could the Russians have helped to poison Yushchenko?

Some people think Yushchenko was not poisoned at all. Scientists point out that dioxin doesn't act overnight. It takes several weeks for symptoms to show up. It's unlikely, then, that Yushchenko was poisoned that night at dinner. He may have been given doses of dioxin over time. But dioxin only kills over a period of years. If a killer wanted to get rid of Yushchenko, why choose dioxin?

Yushchenko still insists he was poisoned. The truth may never be known.

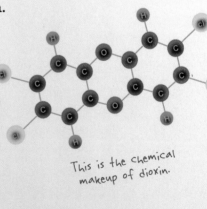

This is the chemical makeup of dioxin.

This isn't the first time that poison might have been given to a politician. Find out about another unsolved toxicology mystery.

The Case of the Royal Poisoning

French Emperor Napoleon Bonaparte dies after a strange illness. Can a 200-year-old lock of hair solve this historical mystery?

May 15, 1821
St. Helena
off the coast of Africa

A History Mystery

For six years, Napoleon suffered from strange symptoms. Was someone poisoning him?

Napoleon Bonaparte spent the last six years of his life in pain. The French emperor had once ruled half of Europe. He led large armies who obeyed his commands. He challenged the governments of Italy, Egypt, and Russia. He won nearly every battle he fought.

But in 1815, Napoleon surrendered to the British army. The British sent Napoleon to an African island

Napoleon was once the most powerful man in Europe. But he spent his final years in exile. The British sent him to St. Helena, an island off the coast of Africa. There, he died a slow and painful death. Nearly 200 years later, people are still trying to find out why.

garloaf Pt.

Flagstaff Bay

W

S

ATLANTIC OCEAN

asture Pt.

cot

Lon

St. Matthew Cathedral

Mt. Actaeon

Blue Hill Village

Southwest Pt.

AFRICA

SOUTH AMERICA

ST. HELENA

ATLANTIC OCEAN

Stove Top Bay

Manati

Deep Valley

AN EMPEROR'S LIFE

Here's a quick look at the life of Napoleon Bonaparte

1769: Napoleon is born.

1796: Napoleon takes command of the French army and invades Italy.

1798: Napoleon conquers Egypt.

1799: Napoleon becomes ruler of France.

1804: Napoleon crowns himself Emperor of the French.

1805: Napoleon names himself king of Italy. He defeats the Russians and the Austrians.

1808: The French army defeats Sweden. Napoleon now controls most of Europe.

1812: Napoleon leads an army into Russia. After four months, he is forced to retreat.

1814: Napoleon's enemies invade France. Napoleon is forced to surrender. He is sent to the island of Elba.

1815: Napoleon escapes. He takes command of Paris. But in June, his army is crushed by the British. He is sent to St. Helena.

May 5, 1821: Napoleon dies after six years on St. Helena.

called St. Helena. He was to stay there for the rest of his life—which turned out to be miserable.

Napoleon arrived in St. Helena in 1815. His health quickly started to fail. For about six years, he battled a strange illness. His legs swelled. He complained of aches and pains. He had serious headaches, diarrhea, and vomiting. He couldn't sleep.

A painting of Napoleon from about 1803. He appears to be in good health.

Napoleon insisted he was being poisoned. His doctors believed he had stomach cancer or a liver problem. Finally, in May 1821, the former emperor died. His grave was dug on St. Helena. Was the truth about his death buried with his body?

Case Reopened

What really happened to Napoleon? Does modern science have the answer?

During his lifetime, Napoleon failed to convince people that he was being poisoned. More than 130 years later, a Swedish dentist began to think the emperor was right.

Dr. Sten Forshufvud was a big fan of Napoleon. He loved to read about the emperor's life. In 1955, a publisher printed the **memoir** of one of Napoleon's friends. It described every terrible day of Napoleon's final month.

Another painting of Napoleon in healthier days. This one was painted around 1812.

Forshufvud read the book with interest. But something didn't seem right. Historians said Napoleon died of stomach cancer. But his symptoms didn't sound like cancer. Forshufvud looked up **arsenic** poisoning in a medical dictionary. Nearly all the symptoms matched Napoleon's illness.

The dentist remembered another detail. In 1840, officials decided to move Napoleon's grave to France. They dug up the emperor's body. When the casket was opened, the body looked strangely well preserved. Arsenic can have that effect.

Could it be that arsenic killed Napoleon—then kept his body from rotting? To answer that question, Forshufvud needed a piece of the emperor.

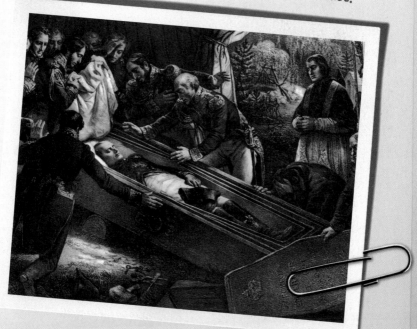

Napoleon's body at St. Helena is prepared for its return to France.

Hair-Raising Tests

How do you test for poison in a 130-year-old body?

Forshufvud knew what he had to do. He spent three years looking for samples of Napoleon's hair. He got some help from a common 19th-century tradition. The day after Napoleon died, his hair was shaved off. Friends and family members kept the locks as a way of remembering their loved one.

Forshufvud managed to buy some of the emperor's hair from collectors. The dentist had all the evidence he needed. Now the question was: Did the hair contain traces of arsenic? If so, how much? And when did the poison enter Emperor Napoleon's body?

Forshufvud sent the strands to Dr. Hamilton Smith in England. Smith had developed a way to measure toxins in hair.

Smith's method involves splitting the hair sample into tiny particles. The particles can then be analyzed using a device called a **spectrometer**.

Smith's spectrometer showed exactly what Forshufvud expected. Napoleon had a high level of arsenic in his body.

Smith and Forshufvud weren't done yet. They wanted to know exactly when the levels of arsenic in Napoleon's body rose. They figured that hair grows an inch (2.5 cm) every two months. The strands in their sample were three inches long. These hairs represented the last six months of Napoleon's life.

The scientists divided the hair into sections. They measured the arsenic in each section. They found that during some weeks Napoleon took in large amounts of arsenic. During other weeks, the amounts were much smaller.

Now they compared their results to the memoir. Did Napoleon's health in the final weeks of his life match the arsenic levels? The two timelines matched perfectly. Napoleon had been miserable when arsenic levels were high. His health improved when the levels were low.

Smith and Forshufvud were ready to make their conclusion. In 1961, they published their findings. Napoleon, they said, had been murdered.

A piece of Napoleon's hair, stuck to a document. The document is written in French. It says that one of Napoleon's servants, Abraham Noverraz, took this hair from Napoleon's head after he died.

Killer Wallpaper?

Could it be the murderer wasn't a person at all?

A lot of people were not convinced that Napoleon had been poisoned. But Ben Weider became a true believer. Weider is a millionaire businessman from Canada. He is also extremely interested in Napoleon.

After Forshufvud announced his results, Weider spent the next four decades researching Napoleon. He read everything he could find about the emperor. He searched far and wide for more hair samples. When he found them, he paid for new tests.

POISON ALERT
What is arsenic, and what does it do to the body?

There's arsenic in your body right now. How'd it get there? Arsenic is a metal. It can be found in rocks, soil, even the air. Drinking water often contains small amounts of the poison.

Arsenic is also added to many products. It helps keep building materials—like wood—from rotting. It's used in some paints, dyes, drugs, and soaps. It's also added to pesticides and weed killers.

Everyone is exposed to low levels of arsenic. For most people, that's not a problem. In high doses, however, arsenic can be very dangerous. It can cause cancer or skin disease. It can also damage the liver and kidneys.

In 1995, Weider had the FBI test new hair samples. In 2001, he sent five more strands to a French team. Both tests found high levels of poison in the samples. The French team said Napoleon had seven to 38 times more arsenic in him than is normal.

But did the poison really come from a murderer?

Ben Weider is president of the International Napoleonic Society. He is holding his book, Was Napoleon Poisoned?

Some people think Napoleon took in the arsenic little by little during his daily life. In the 1880s, many products were made with arsenic. Shampoos and other hair products had arsenic in them. Some medicines contained small amounts of the poison. Some colored dyes were made with arsenic.

According to one theory, Napoleon was killed by his wallpaper. A series of strange deaths in the 1800s puzzled doctors. In 1893, the deaths were traced to a green dye used in wallpaper. The dye had high levels of arsenic in it. In damp rooms, it formed a mold that was highly toxic.

On St. Helena, Napoleon often took long, steamy

baths to relax. What was one of the colors in his bathroom wallpaper? Green.

Was one of the most powerful men in history killed by his wallpaper? Or did someone poison him slowly and secretly? No one knows for sure.

Some people still insist that stomach cancer was the real killer. They say there's no way to prove that the hair samples Ben Weider used came from Napoleon.

Weider wants to dig up the emperor's body to make sure. Until then, the truth will probably stay buried.

The green dye in Napoleon's wallpaper had high levels of arsenic in it. Could that have killed him? This paper was taken from one of the rooms in Napoleon's house on St. Helena. You can see the green dye outlining the designs.

FORENSIC
DOWNLOAD

Here's even more amazing stuff about forensic toxicology for you to swallow.

400s B.C. A Deadly Cure

The Greek doctor Hippocrates *(left)* used arsenic to treat stomach problems. That's pretty weird when you realize that he was also famous for his motto, which is now called the Hippocratic Oath. That motto includes the promise to "Do no harm."

Key Dates in Forensic Toxicology

1850 Detecting Poison

French scientist Jean Servois Stas invented a way to find poison in a victim's body. A victim had died of chemical burns in his mouth. Stas poured **ether**, a type of alcohol, on the victim's tissues. The ether evaporated and the drug was left behind. It was **nicotine**, the chemical used in cigarettes. Stas helped prove that the killer forced the victim to eat tobacco.

1906 Color Coded

Russian plant scientist Alexandr Tswett found a new way to identify chemicals. It's called paper **chromatography**. The process separates small amounts of substances from one another. Each substance creates a different colored band on paper. Scientists study that band to learn about the substance. Today, toxicologists use a similar method to test for chemicals.

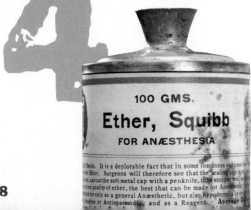

100 GMS.
Ether, Squibb
FOR ANÆSTHESIA

Oxide. It is a deplorable fact that in some instances our cans are
Ether. Surgeons will therefore see that the sealing sap is not
cut out the soft metal cap with a penknife, than stopper well w
quality of ether, the best that can be made for Anæsthesia
used not only as a general Anæsthetic, but also hypodermically
odyne or Antispasmodic, and as a Reagent. Average Do

399 B.C. First Famous Poisoning

Greek rulers sentenced the philosopher Socrates to death by poisoning. The charge? Corrupting the minds of young people. Socrates (*above, center*) was given a drink made with the deadly poison **hemlock**.

1752 Science in Court

An English court sentenced Mary Blandy (*below*) to death by hanging for poisoning her father. She had wanted to marry a Scottish captain—against her father's wishes. The captain sent Mary a powder, which she spread on her father's food. At the trial, scientists testified that the powder was arsenic. Their evidence? It looked and smelled like arsenic. Blandy's trial was the first to use toxicology as evidence.

Poisons have been used to kill since ancient times. Check out this timeline about the world's poisonous past.

1950s Toxicology Takes Off

Forensic toxicologists got new high-tech tools. Ultraviolet lights, x-rays, and gas chromatographs helped them track down hard-to-find poisons.

2004 Poisoned Politician?

Ukranian presidential candidate Viktor Yushchenko claimed he was poisoned by his opponents. He went on to win the election.

Name Your Poison

Have a look at some of the equipment and forms used by forensic toxicologists. And find out what to do if you suspect a child has been poisoned.

EQUIPMENT

Say toxicologists suspect that someone has drugs in his or her system. There are countless possibilities. To figure out which drug it is, toxicologists often have to do at least two levels of tests: screening and confirming.

Screening tests show that some kind of drug or toxin is mostly likely present.

Confirming tests are more sensitive and can confirm the presence of a poison.

Here's a look at some of these tests.

SCREENING

IMMUNOASSAY TEST
This test can **detect** certain kinds of drugs in the body. **Immunoassay** of urine samples can detect aspirin. It can also detect barbiturates, a kind of drug that calms people down and can even put them to sleep. And it can detect cocaine and other narcotic drugs.

THIN-LAYER CHROMATOGRAPH
This test can separate out all the various parts of a chemical. It can test for hundreds of different substances at once.

CONFIRMING

GAS CHROMATOGRAPH WITH MASS SPECTROMETRY
The gas chromatograph can separate the sample into all its chemical parts. The mass spectrometry can then identify all these parts.

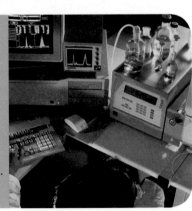

POISONING FACT SHEET

What should I do if I think a child has been poisoned?
Call your local poison center right away. Do not wait for the child to look or feel sick! Follow these first-aid steps:

■ **Swallowed Poisons**
- Do not give the victim anything to eat or drink before calling the poison center or a doctor.
- Do not make the child throw up or give ipecac syrup unless a doctor or the poison center tells you to.

■ **Inhaled Poisons**
- Get the victim to fresh air right away. Call the poison center.

■ **Poisons on the Skin**
- Remove contaminated clothing and rinse the child's skin with water for 10 minutes. Call the poison center.

■ **Poisons in the Eye**
- Flush the child's eye for 15 minutes using a large cup filled with lukewarm water held 2–4 inches (5–10 cm) from the eye. Call the poison center.

For more poison prevention and first aid information or
to locate your local poison center, visit the American Association of
Poison Control Centers Web site at: www.aapcc.org

This sheet is made available through the financial support of
Health Resources and Services Administration Maternal
Child Health Bureau.

Boxes 1 Through 6 MUST BE COMPLETED **Drug Analysis Request Form**

(1) Type of Case (Check Proper Box in Each Column)

Type of Case
- ☐ Fatal Accident
- ☐ P.I. Accident
- ☐ P.D. Accident
- ☐ Homicide
- ☐ OWI
- ☐ Suicide
- ☐ Other (Specify)_____

Status of Subject
- ☐ Dead
- ☐ Injured
- ☐ Not Injured

Medical examiners or police officers fill out forms like this one. Such forms tell toxicologists exactly what to look for.

(2) Subject Information   Lab Case #

Name of Subject (Last, First, Mi... ...ial)

Street Address

The victim's name and other information goes here.

...le ☐ Female

(3) Submitting Agency

Inves... ing Officer/Coroner   Agency

Investigators, police officers, or medical examiners put their information here. It tells toxicologists who is requesting the testing.

...cy Case #

...y of Occurrence

URI #

(4) Collection Data and Chain of Custody Information

Specimen Taken By:_____   Loca...

Date Taken: _____   Time Taken: _____   am W...

Received From _____   Released To _____

Received From _____   Released To _____

Received From _____   Released To _____

Received From _____   Released To _____

This section is important—especially in court. The chain of custody tracks who handled the evidence and when. It starts when an officer or a medical examiner finds a sample. After that, every time evidence changes hands, it must be recorded. The fewer people in the chain of custody, the better. Every time people handle a piece of evidence, they can damage it.

This section tells toxicologists if the victim was given a breath test for alcohol.

(5) Breath Test

Was a valid chemical breath test administered by a certified operator as defined in PL 143-1983 and ICS 11-4-5? ☐ Yes ☐ No

(6) Drug Requests

The investigators who order the toxicology test decide what drugs to test for. They also check off the type of sample: blood, urine, or other (such as tissues or organs).

Drug Panel	Drugs ...
Alcohol	Ethanol
Drug Screen I	Barbiturates, Benzodiazepines, Cannabinoids, Cocaine, and Opiates
Drug Screen II	Screen I + Amphetamines, Methadone, Phencyclidine, and Propoxyphene
Single Class Drug Screen	Specify (Drug Classes Listed Above) _____ ☐ Blood ☐ Urine
Other Drug Requests	Specify _____

All Positive blood ethanol results will ... other drug classes, confirmatory ... the presence and to quantif...

This section gives investigators step-by-step instructions on how to handle evidence and samples. It also explains how to take samples from a victim.

(7) Instructions

Instructions to Investigating Officer:

1. Fill out the Drug Analysis Request Form completely and legibly.
2. Witness the collection of the samples.
   A. Blood should be collected in the gray stoppered tubes.
   B. Urine should be collected in the specimen bottle.
3. Fill out all information requested on the blood tube label(s) and/or urine bottle label.
4. Return filled blood tubes to the styrofoam holder.
5. Place styrofoam holder an...

DO NOT remove...

6. Affix evidence seal to zipl...
7. Place completed Drug An...
8. Reassemble kit box and ...
9. Send specimens (blood, ...
   Indi...
   635...
   Indi...

Instructions to Physician or Technician

1. Clean skin with non-alco...
2. Draw blood with a clean...
3. If drawing blood with a s...
4. To ensure proper mixing...
   (Do Not Shake Vigorous...
5. "Location" refers to the ...

American Board of Forensic Toxicology Guidelines

6.4 Recommended Amounts of Specimens

Many deaths involve ingestion of multiple drugs, necessitating larger amounts of tissue and fluids to be collected at autopsy for toxicological examination. The following is a suggested list of specimens and amounts to be collected at autopsy in such cases:

Brain: 50 gm
Liver: 50 gm
Kidney: 50 gm
Heart blood: 25 ml
Peripheral blood: 10 ml
Vitreous humor: all available
Bile: all available
Urine: all available
Gastric contents: all available

Help Wanted: Forensic Toxicologist

Can you picutre yourself as a forensic toxicologist?
Here's more information about the field.

Q&A: DR. DAVID VIDAL

David Vidal is a senior criminalist for the Los Angeles County Sheriff's Department in California.

Q Why did you decide to become a forensic toxicologist?

Vidal: I started out in a hospital lab, which is very different from a crime lab. I jumped into forensic toxicology because it's a more interesting and exciting job.

Q What's the best part about your job?

Vidal: The lab work. I like analyzing things and working on machines. It's nice when we get unexpected results.

Q Can you solve a case in one hour, like they do on crime scene shows?

Vidal: Not really. But some of the cases that we've worked on in our lab show up on *CSI*. Some of our retired lab people work with the show.

Q What kind of cases do you normally work on?

Vidal: We usually test for drugs in blood and urine. But sometimes we get poisoning cases. They might involve food-tampering or poison in liquids. Another case might be pet poisoning, where someone stuffs pills into a raw hamburger and throws it over the fence for the neighbor's dog. Another case might involve testing vomit for a dangerous club drug.

Q What's the hardest part?

Vidal: Most people would probably say testifying in court. It's a lot of pressure. You have to be tough-minded and thick-skinned. But the work that we do is important for society, for court, for victims of a crime, and for the accused.

Q What's your advice for people who are thinking about a career in forensic toxicology?

Vidal: [Work hard in] high school and college. You'll need a degree in a hard science, such as chemistry, biology, biochemistry, or microbiology. Besides studying hard, it's a good idea to get involved and do volunteer work at a crime lab. You'll get to learn about the real world from the inside.

THE STATS

Day Job
Most forensic toxicologists work in crime labs for city, county, or state governments. The FBI and other federal agencies have their own forensic toxicology labs. Forensic toxicologists can also work for hospitals and sports agencies that test for drugs and steroids in athletes.

Money
$45,000–$100,000

Education
Forensic toxicologists must finish the following:
- ▶ 4 years of college
- ▶ graduate school to receive a master's or doctoral degree
- ▶ certification by the American Board of Forensic Toxicology

The Numbers
The international association of forensic toxicologists has 1,400 members worldwide.

DO YOU HAVE WHAT IT TAKES?

Take this totally unscientific quiz to find out if forensic toxicology might be a good career for you.

1. **Toxicologists work with chemicals and dead bodies—which can have strong smells. How do you feel about sniffing odors all day?**
   a) No problem. That's what noses are for!
   b) I prefer to smell flowers, but I can put up with nasty scents.
   c) Gross! Take me to the nearest perfume counter!

2. **As a forensic toxicologist, you'll be handling blood, urine, and body tissues. Would you mind that?**
   a) Bring me those latex gloves! I can't wait to test this stuff in a lab.
   b) I'm a bit freaked out by blood, but I might be able to handle it.
   c) Keep that away from me!

3. **How are you with following directions?**
   a) I follow directions step-by-step and check my work.
   b) I try to follow directions most of the time, but sometimes I might skip a step.
   c) I don't like following directions. I prefer to wing it.

4. **When I want to learn more about something, I:**
   a) ask questions, search the Internet, read books about it.
   b) ask my friends.
   c) go back to sleep.

5. **How do you feel about speaking in front of a group of people?**
   a) I'm comfortable making a presentation in front of a crowd.
   b) I'm a bit shy and not very confident when people focus on me.
   c) I try to avoid it as much as possible.

YOUR SCORE

Give yourself 3 points for every "**a**" you chose.

Give yourself 2 points for every "**b**" you chose.

Give yourself 1 point for every "**c**" you chose.

If you got **13–15 points**, you'd probably be a good forensic toxicologist.

If you got **10–12 points**, you might be a good forensic toxicologist.

If you got **5–9 points**, you might want to look at another career!

HOW TO GET STARTED...NOW!

It's never too early to start working toward your goals.

GET AN EDUCATION

▶ Focus on your science classes, such as chemistry and biology.

▶ Start thinking about college. Look for ones with good biochemistry and pharmacology programs.

▶ Read the newspaper. Keep up with what's going on in your community.

▶ Read anything you can find about forensic toxicology. See the books and Web sites in the Resources section on pages 108–112.

▶ Graduate from high school!

NETWORK!

▶ Find out about forensic groups in your area.

▶ See if you can find a local toxicologist who might be willing to give you advice. Or look for someone on the Web.

GET AN INTERNSHIP

▶ Look for an internship with a toxicologist.

▶ Look for an internship in a local forensic lab.

LEARN ABOUT OTHER JOBS IN THE FIELD

▶ criminalist

▶ biochemist

▶ forensic biologist

Resources

Looking for more information about criminal profiling and forensic toxicology? Here are some resources you don't want to miss!

Professional Organizations

Academy of Behavioral Profiling (ABP)
www.profiling.org/abp_about.html
Academy of Behavioral Profiling
336 Lincoln Street, P.O. Box 6406
Sitka, AK 99835
PHONE: 831-254-5446

The ABP is a professional organization that promotes education and training for criminal profilers.

American Academy of Forensic Sciences (AAFS)
www.aafs.org
410 North 21st Street
Colorado Springs, CO 80904-2798
PHONE: 719-636-1100

The AAFS is an organization for forensic scientists. It helps them meet and share information with other forensic experts. The AAFS sponsors seminars and conferences.

Canadian Society of Forensic Science (CSFS)

www.csfs.ca
P.O. Box 37040
3332 McCarthy Road
Ottawa, Ontario
Canada K1V 0W0
PHONE: 613-738-0001
E-MAIL: csfs@bellnet.ca

This nonprofit organization promotes the study of forensic science. Its Web site has information about careers and schools with forensic programs.

Forensic Toxicologist Certification Board, Inc.
http://home.usit.net/~robsears/ftcb/index.htm
P.O. Box 21398
Columbia, SC 29221-1398
PHONE: 803-896-7365
FAX: 803-896-7542

The Forensic Toxicologist Certification Board was established in 1992.

International Association of Forensic Toxicologists
www.tiaft.org
211 East Chicago Ave.
Chicago, IL 60611-2678
PHONE: 312-440-2500

The International Association of Forensic Toxicologists is 45 years old. It works to promote cooperation among members and to encourage research in forensic toxicology.

Society of Forensic Toxicologists, Inc. (SOFT)
www.soft-tox.org
P.O. Box 5543
Mesa, AZ 85211-5543
PHONE/FAX: 480-839-9106

SOFT is an organization made up of practicing forensic toxicologists who are interested in promoting and developing forensic toxicology.

Education and Training

The AAFS Web site (**www.aafs.org**) has a list of colleges and universities with forensic science programs.

Federal Bureau of Investigation (FBI)

www.fbi.gov/
J. Edgar Hoover Building
935 Pennsylvania Avenue, NW
Washington, DC 20535-0001
PHONE: 210-567-3177
E-MAIL: smile@uthscsa.edu

The FBI Web site contains information on its latent print unit. Its Behavioral Science Unit also gives information on getting a job with the FBI (click on "training").

Royal Canadian Mounted Police (RCMP)

www.rcmp-grc.gc.ca/ techops/recruiting_e.htm
RCMP Headquarters
1200 Vanier Parkway
Ottawa, Ontario
Canada K1A 0R2
PHONE: 613-993-7267

The RCMP is the Canadian national police service. Its Web site gives information on different jobs within the RCMP, including the investigative behavioral sciences programs.

Web Sites

American Board of Forensic Toxicology
www.abft.org

This Web site offers information and links for toxicologists. Offers lab accreditation.

California Association of Toxicologists
www.cal-tox.org

This Web site includes space for members to communicate and recent publications on the study of toxicology.

Center for Investigative Psychology
www.i-psy.com

This Web site gives information about conferences and provides links to recent published studies in the field.

truTV's Crime Library
www.crimelibrary.com

For a variety of information about forensic science.

Environmental Criminology Research, Inc.
www.ecricanada.com

The Web site for this company contains information on geographic profiling.

The Evidence: A Forensic Science Technology Journal
www.theevidence.ca

This is a Web site that publishes research being done in toxicology and other forensic sciences.

Forensic Solutions, LLC
www.corpus-delicti.com

The Web site for this company contains information on profiling, suggested reading, and a list of helpful resources.

Books

Camenson, Blythe. *Opportunities in Forensic Science Careers.* New York; McGraw-Hill, 2001.
This book has information about training, education, salaries, and career opportunities in the field of forensic science.

Campbell, Andrea. *Crime Scene (Detective Notebook).* New York: Sterling, 2004.
Kids will learn about what it really takes to bring criminals to justice: what good evidence is, how to use memory and observation, and what an important role science plays.

Dahl, Michael. *Computer Evidence (Forensic Crime Solvers).* Kentwood, La.: Edge Books, 2004.
This book looks at solving crimes in cyberspace.

Donkin, Andrew. *Crime Busters.* New York: DK Publishing, 2001.
Kids will learn how law enforcement masterminds catch the criminals.

Emsley, John. *The Elements of Murder: A History of Poison.* New York: Oxford University Press, 2005.

Esherick, Joan. *Criminal Psychology and Personality Profiling.* Broomall, Pa.: Mason Crest Publishers, 2005.
This book explains how profilers come up with their suspects.

Evans, Colin. *The Casebook of Forensic Detection: How Science Solved 100 of the World's Most Baffling Crimes.* Indianapolis: Wiley, 1999.

Fisher, Barry A. J. *Techniques of Crime Scene Investigation, 7th ed.* Boca Raton, Fla.: CRC Press, 2003.
This is an introduction to the techniques real crime scene investigators use.

Genge, Ngaire, E. *The Forensic Casebook: The Science of Crime Scene Investigation.* New York: Ballantine, 2002.
This book looks at all kinds of forensic crime-fighting. It also has information on jobs and training programs.

Innes, Brian. *The Search for Forensic Evidence.* Milwaukee: Gareth Stevens Publishing, 2005.

James, Stuart, and Jon J. Nordby. *Forensic Science: An Introduction to Scientific and Investigative Techniques, 2nd ed.* Boca Raton, Fla.: CRC Books, 2005.

Macinnis, Peter. *Poisons: From Hemlock to Botox to the Killer Bean of Calabar.* New York: Arcade Publishing, 2005.

Platt, Richard. *Crime Scene: Ultimate Guide to Forensic Science*. New York: DK Publishing, 2006.
This book takes a look at the latest high-tech tools being used in forensic science.

Platt, Richard. *Forensics.* Boston: Kingfisher, 2005.

Rainis, Kenneth G. *Crime-Solving Science Projects: Forensic Science Experiments*. Berkeley Heights, N.J.: Enslow Publishing, 2000.
Students learn about fingerprints, fibers, blood evidence, and other factors of forensic science.

Smith, Fred. *Handbook of Forensic Drug Analysis.* Burlington, Mass.: Academic Press, 2004.

Trestrail, John Harris. *Criminal Poisoning: Investigational Guide for Law Enforcement, Toxicologists, Forensic Scientists, and Attorneys.* Totowa, N.J.: Humana Press, 2000.

Turkington, Carol. *The Poisons and Antidotes Sourcebook, 2nd ed.* New York: Checkmark Books, 1999.

Walker, Pam, and Elaine Wood. *Crime Scene Investigations: Real-Life Science Labs for Grades 6–12*. New York: Jossey-Bass, 1998.
Find step-by-step experiments so kids can solve crimes just like real forensic scientists.

A

acute (uh-KYOOT) *adjective* describing something that is quick and intense. An acute poisoning is serious and happens very fast.

AFIS (AY-fis) *noun* a computer database in which police store the prints of arrested suspects. AFIS stands for *Automated Fingerprint Identification System*.

agent (AY-juhnt) *noun* a person trained to do a job for a company or government organization

arsenic (AHR-suh-nik) *noun* a metallic poison found in wood preservatives and other products

autopsy (AW-top-see) *noun* an examination of a body to determine how and why a person died

B

behavior (bih-HAYV-yer) *noun* the way a person acts or responds to certain conditions. Behavioral sciences are sciences that study the ways people behave.

bile (byle) *noun* a liquid produced by the liver that can show what toxins are in someone's body

C

chain of custody (chayn uhv KUH-stuh-dee) *noun* a list of people who handle evidence. The fewer people who handle the samples, the better. In court, lawyers can attack toxicology tests if sample evidence is not handled properly.

characteristics (ka-rik-tuh-RISS-tiks) *noun* qualities, features, or marks that help identify something

chemical (KEM-i-cull) *noun* a human-made substance created from two or more materials

chromatography (kro-muh-TAH-graff-ee) *noun* a laboratory test that separates every material in a substance or chemical

chronic (KRAH-nik) *adjective* describing something that happens over time. A chronic poisoning occurs gradually and in small doses.

CODIS (KOH-diss) *noun* a database that contains DNA samples of more than 300,000 people. It stands for *Combined DNA Index System*.

coma (KOH-muh) *noun* a state of deep sleep (unconsciousness) caused by disease or illness

conscious (KON-shush) *adjective* awake or aware of what is going on. An unconscious person is alive but cannot hear or see anything.

consultant (kun-SUL-tant) *noun* an expert who charges a fee to provide advice or services in a particular field

convict (con-VIKT) *verb* to find guilty in a court of law

criminal profiling (KRIM-uh-nul PRO-file-ing) *noun* the process of using evidence from a crime scene and knowledge of psychology to predict a criminal's characteristics and personality. Also known as "psychological crime scene analysis."

criminology (KRIM-un-OL-uh-gee) *noun* the scientific study of crime, criminals, criminal behavior, and corrections. A criminologist is an expert in criminology.

cyanide (SYe-uh-nyde) *noun* a fatal poison that is found in dyes, insect killers, and other products

cyberspace (SYE-bur-spayss) *noun* the whole communications universe available on a computer. The prefix *cyber-* refers to that computer world.

D

dastardly (DAS-tard-lee) *adjective* being cowardly and dishonest

database (DAY-tuh-bayss) *noun* a lot of information organized on a computer

detect (di-TEKT) *verb* to notice or discover something

device (di-VYSSE) *noun* a piece of equipment for a certain job

dioxin (DYE-ohk-sun) *noun* a deadly chemical that is used in the manufacture of plastics, paper, and pesticides

DNA (DEE-en-ay) *noun* a chemical found in almost every cell of your body. It's a blueprint for the way you look and function.

drug (druhg) *noun* a natural product or human-made chemical that can change the way the body works

E

ether (EE-thur) *noun* a type of alcohol often used to help dissolve other materials

evidence (EHV-uh-denss) *noun* things that help prove someone is guilty or innocent

expert (EX-purt) *noun* someone who knows a lot about a subject. See pages 14 and 64 for a list of forensic experts.

F

FBI (EF-bee-eye) *noun* a part of the U.S. government that investigates major crimes. It stands for *Federal Bureau of Investigation*.

forensic (fuh-REN-zik) *adjective* relating to a kind of science used to help investigate crimes

H

hack (hak) *verb* to illegally break into a computer system; a person who does this is a hacker

hemlock (HEM-lok) *noun* a poisonous plant or a deadly drink made from that plant

homicide (HOM-uh-side) *noun* a common law enforcement term for murder

I

ID (EYE-dee) *noun* the process of figuring out who someone is. It's short for *identification*.

immunoassay (IH-myoo-noh-ah-SAY) *noun* a test that detects if certain substances are in a person's body and, if so, how much there is

ISP (EYE-ess-pee) *noun* a company that supplies Internet service. It's short for *Internet service provider*.

IT (eye-TEE) *noun* a department that helps keep computers running smoothly. It's short for *information technology*.

J

jury (JUR-ee) *noun* a group of people who listen to a court case and decide if someone is guilty or innocent

M

ME (EM-ee) *noun* a medical doctor who investigates suspicious deaths. It is short for *medical examiner*.

memoir (MEM-whar) *noun* a book that a person writes about his or her own life

MO (EM-oh) *noun* it's short for *modus operandi*, which means "method of operation." It's how a criminal operates.

motive (MOH-tiv) *noun* the reason for doing something. Criminal profilers look for the perp's motive for committing the crime.

N

nicotine (NIK-uh-teen) *noun* a poisonous substance found in tobacco

P

paranoia (PAIR-ah-noy-uh) *noun* a disorder in which someone becomes extremely suspicious of everyone else

perp (purp) *noun* a common law enforcement term for a person who commits a crime. It's short for the word *perpetrator*.

pesticide (PEST-uh-side) *noun* a chemical that kills insects

poison (POY-zuhn) *verb* to give someone any substance that causes injury, illness, or death

predator (PRED-uh-tur) *noun* someone who tries to hurt others

professor (pruh-FESS-ur) *noun* a teacher at a college or university

prosecutor (PROSS-uh-kyoo-tur) *noun* a lawyer who represents the government in criminal trials

psychology (sye-KOL-uh-gee) *noun* the scientific study of the human mind and human behavior

S

serial (SEER-ee-ul) *adjective* done repeatedly or in a series

server (SUR-vur) *noun* a computer in a network that helps the other computers run

signature (SIG-nuh-chur) *noun* a characteristic mark

spectometer (spek-TOM-uh-tur) *noun* a device used to study tiny particles

staging (STAY-jing) *noun* the way items are arranged or placed at a crime scene

stats (stats) *noun* official numbers about events that have happened in the past. It's short for *statistics*.

suspect (SUHS-pekt) *noun* a person law enforcement officials think might be guilty of a crime

symptom (SIMP-tum) *noun* a sign of illness or some physical problem

T

technology (tek-NOL-uh-jee) *noun* the development of new machines, devices, or techniques

theory (THEE-ur-ee) *noun* an idea that explains how something could have happened

toxic (TOK-sik) *adjective* poisonous

toxicology (TOK-sik-ahl-uh-jee) *noun* the science of finding, treating, or studying poisons, drugs, and chemicals

toxin (TOK-sihn) *noun* any substance that can kill cells or cause injury or death. A poison.

V

VICAP (VYE-kap) *noun* a database that contains lots of information about terrible crimes. It's short for *Violent Criminal Apprehension Program*.

victim (VIK-tuhm) *noun* a person who has been hurt, mistreated, or killed

victimology (vik-tim-AH-luh-jee) *noun* the study of how people become victims, or targets of crimes

Index

Photo Credits

Photographs © 2007: AP/Wide World Photos: 41 (Michael Heinz), 49 top (John Youngbear), 95 (Jacques Brinon), 83 (Sergei Chuzavkov), 107 (Charles Dharapak), 70 (Jay LaPrete), 82 (Efrem Lukatsky), 79 (Viktor Pobedinsky/Efrem Lukatsky), 93 (Christian Lutz); Assay Designs, Inc., Ann Arbor, MI: 100 top; Corbis Images: 39 (Roger Ball), 21, 27 top, 47 top (Bettmann), 52 (Chris Collins), 16 bottom, 50 top (Ashley Cooper), 49 bottom (N. Lammer/Oakland Tribune/Sygma), 18 (Michael Ochs Archives), 17 (Charles E. Rotkin), 37 (Rudy Sulgan), 6 top (William Whitehurst), 91 (Bettmann), 75 (DK Limited), 7 center, 84 (Igor Kostin), 72 bottom (James Leynse), 67 (Greg Probst), 87; truTV: 48 bottom; Courtesy of Dayle Hinman: 16 top, 32, 33, 48 top, 53; Dr. Maurice Godwin: 55; Florida State Department of Corrections: 35; ForensicDentalServices/www.forensicdentistryonline.org: 51; Getty Images: 23 bottom (Frederic Lewis), 50 bottom (Mark Scott), 29 (Micheal Simpson), 22, 23 top, 27 bottom (Peter Stackpole), 31 (David Toase), 109 (Mark Wilson), 77 (Jerry Alexander), 85 (Graeme Robertson); Courtesy Gregg Olsen, author of *Bitter Almonds: The True Story of Mothers, Daughters, and the Seattle Cyanide Murders*: 73 top, 74; Indiana State Department of Toxicology: 102, 103; James Levin Studios: 4, 6 bottom left, 10, 12, 60; Marc Rogers: 5 bottom, 40, 54; Mary Evans Picture Library: 98 top, 99 bottom; Photo Researchers, NY: 5 center, 6 bottom right, 8 top, 36 (Michael Donne), 57 (Tek Image), 62 (Scott Camazine), 86 (James Cavallini), 81 (Mark Thomas), 100 bottom (G. Tompkinson), 100 center (Charles D. Winters); Sirchie Fingerprint Laboratories: 27 inset, 56, 106; Superstock, Inc./Bill Barley: 68; The Art Archive/Picture Desk: 7 bottom, 90 (Dagli Orti/Musée Carnavalet Paris), 89 (Dagli Orti/Musée du Château de Versailles); The Granger Collection New York: 99 top; The Image Works: 46 top (Public Record Office/HIP), 5 top, 7 top (Al Campanie/Syracuse Newspapers), 8 bottom, 28 (Topham), 98 bottom, 110 (Science Museum/SSPL); The Picture Desk: 46 bottom (John Meek/The Art Archive), 47 bottom (Universal/Kobal Collection); Toni Vidal: 104; Courtesy of Victor Blair, Napoleonic Historian, The Napoleon Series: 96. Maps by David Lindroth, Inc.

Writing this book has turned me into a scientific sleuth. It's difficult to track down information regarding poisoning cases. Because most poisoning cases involve a victim, a murderer, or court, getting people to discuss a case is tough work.

Luckily, there's lots of information on the Internet, in toxicology journals, and in books. And toxicologists are more than happy to share information about their scientific field—as long as you don't show their names or faces in the book!

The majority of toxicologists work for city, county, or state-run crime labs. Because these toxicologists testify in court, their credibility might be compromised if their names, photos, and other information are splashed across a book. To avoid this problem, I've had to use anonymous helpers to gather information.

—D.B. Beres

Like a lot of people, I was a big fan of the criminal profilers I saw on TV and in the movies.

Hollywood always seems to play up the "gut instincts" of the investigators, making profilers seem like psychics who know what the killer is thinking. I now know just how much science is behind real criminal profiling.

If you want to learn more about psychological crime scene analysis, follow the trail I took: start with the Web sites listed in the Resources section. If you like reading about cases, try the truTV site.

The sites for professional organizations give info on getting a job in the field. And you can always type "criminal profiling" into the search engine on your computer and get lots of interesting links.

You can also read news articles about famous profiling cases, or check out books by well-known profilers. You can even find profiling textbooks at bookstores, but they can be pretty complicated, so have your dictionary handy!

The big surprise in my research was how much the profiling field is changing and how much controversy surrounds it. There are several teaching methods, each involving a different type of science and research. The field is a lot more complicated than it seems!

I have to say, as cool as the job looks, I could never be a profiler. Just reading all the murder cases made me double-lock my doors!

—Anna Prokos

Acknowledgments

I would like to thank Barry A.J. Fisher and David Vidal (top-secret state toxicologist) for taking the time to talk about their work.

—D.B.B.

I would like to thank the following people and organizations for their time and cooperation. I couldn't have written this book without their help.

Dayle Hinman
Dr. Maurice Godwin
Dr. Marc Rogers
Dr. Robert Keppel
truTV
American Academy of Forensic Sciences

—A.P.

CONTENT ADVISERS:

Christopher Long, PhD, DABFT, Director of St. Louis University Forensic and Environmental Toxicology Laboratories

H.W. "Rus" Ruslander, Forensic Supervisor, Palm Beach County (Florida) Medical Examiner's Office

Donna Brandelli, MFS, Forensic Identification Specialist

NOTES